THE FIRST AND THE LAST

by

William Edwy Vine

1873-1949 M.A.

WIPF & STOCK · Eugene, Oregon

Wipf and Stock Publishers
199 W 8th Ave, Suite 3
Eugene, OR 97401

The First and the Last
By Vine, W. E.
Softcover ISBN-13: 978-1-7252-7942-1
Publication date 4/29/2020
Previously published by Pickering and Inglis, 1920

CONTENTS

Chapter I

The Pre-Existent One, ... 1

His Eternal Pre-Existence—His Own Testimony—The Personal Word—The Testimony of the Epistles—The Testimony of Christ in the Apocalypse.

Chapter II

The Eternal Sonship of Christ, ... 8

God Sent Forth His Son—The Lord's Testimony—The Testimony of John's First Epistle—His Only Begotten Son—The Term, "Begotten"—The Term, "Firstborn"—Human Recognition of His Sonship—The Son Prior to Creation—"He that Confesseth the Son."

Chapter III

The Incarnation of our Lord, ... 18

"The Word Became Flesh"—The Reality of His Manhood—Not the Union of Two Persons—How was the Incarnation Possible?—How was the Incarnation Accomplished?—Essential to the Christian Faith—"The Grace of Our Lord Jesus Christ."

CONTENTS

Chapter IV

The Perfect Servant, ... 27

A Bond-Servant—His Divine Attributes—His Obedience to the Father—His Anointing—He Laid Down His Life—"Of That Day and That Hour"—The Barren Fig Tree—His Example to Us.

Chapter V

The Sinlessness of Christ, ... 38

The Testimony of the Apostles—The Witness of the Gospels—His Character and Ways—Contact Without Contamination—His Own Claims—The Testimony of His Foes—Did He Adapt His Teaching to Human Ignorance?—Inevitable Conclusions.

Chapter VI

The Moral Glories of Christ, ... 48

The Harmony of His Character—The Initial Gospel Records—The Temptations and Their Counterpart—"He That Overcometh"—Heredity—Environment—The Ninefold Fruit.

Chapter VII

The Atoning Sacrifice of Christ, .. 64

Divinely Pre-Ordained—Vicarious—The Character of Sin—The Person Requisite—An Objection—Another Objection—The Nature of His Death—Reconciliation—Redemption—The Scope of the Atonement.

CONTENTS

CHAPTER VIII
The Resurrection of Christ, ... 76
The Vindication of His Divine Sonship—The Ratification of the Atoning Efficacy of His Death—The Basis of the Gospel—The Evidence—The Cloths in the Empty Tomb—The Effect on the Disciples—The Veracity of the Writers—Not Merely a Spiritual Resurrection—The Effects.

CHAPTER IX
The Ascension of Christ, ... 88
The First and the Fourth Gospels—The Gospel of Luke—The Character of the Records—The Place — The Disciples — The Event — The Evidences — The Effects — The Person — The Dispensational Significance.

CHAPTER X
The High Priesthood of Christ, ... 79
The Melchizedek Order—Anticipations in the Days of His Flesh—His Official Glory—His Intercession.

CHAPTER XI
The Second Advent, ... 106
Christ's Own Expectancy—The Day of Christ—The Parousia—The Day of the Lord—The Manifestation of the Parousia—The Marriage and the Marriage Feast—The Judgment of the Nations—The Millennium

"Behold, I come quickly; and My reward is with Me, to render to each man according as his work is. I am the Alpha and the Omega, THE FIRST AND THE LAST, the Beginning and the End" (Rev. 22. 12, 13, R.V.).

The First and the Last
A Study of the Person and Work of Christ.

The Pre-Existent One.

WE may well hesitate to write anything upon the infinitely great and sacred subject of the Person and Work of the Son of God. The place whereon we tread is holy ground; we may not approach it save with unshod feet, lest we make ourselves of the number of those who have desecrated it by erroneous speculations and by perversions of the truth. The apprehension of the numerous onslaughts being made upon the doctrines of the faith concerning our adorable Lord, and the command given us "to contend earnestly for the faith once for all delivered to the saints" (Jude 3), provide additional inducement to handle this holy theme, and so to continue the witness already faithfully given by those who have held and taught the truth.

His Eternal Pre-existence.

In the contemplation of this subject our thoughts are carried by the Scriptures into the measureless eternity of the past, and from thence to what constitutes the period of greatest crisis in the history of the human race, and again onward to the timeless, endless future. Two of these, and sometimes all three, are in some passages put into conjunction. For instance, the prophetic utterance which predicted the locality of the Lord's Incarnation declared at the same time His unoriginated existence in the past eternity: "But thou, Bethlehem Ephratah, which art little to be among the thousands of Judah, out of thee shall One come forth unto Me that is to be ruler in Israel; whose goings forth are from of old, from everlasting" (Micah 5. 2). There can be no mistaking Who is meant. The Person indicated is He who was "born in Bethlehem of Judæa, in the days of Herod the king" (Matt. 2. 1). The chief priests and scribes knew full well that Micah's prophecy spoke directly of the Messiah, for they quoted it in answer to Herod's inquiry where the Christ should be born (vv. 4-6). The phrase, "from everlasting to everlasting," is the same in the original as in the words of the Psalm of Moses, "From everlasting to everlasting Thou art God" (Psa. 90. 2).

His Own Testimony.

Christ Himself declared His eternal preexistence when He said to the Jews: "Verily, verily, I say unto you, Before Abraham was, I am" (John 8. 58). Strictly rendered it is: "Before Abraham came to be, I am." He sets Himself in contrast to Abraham in this, that Abraham's existence had an inception, His own existence was marked by no beginning; Abraham's was limited by the condition of time, His had been eternal. Conscious of His limitless, timeless existence in the past, He speaks of Himself by the eternal title of Jehovah, the great "I AM." The Jews had no misunderstanding about that. The discussion closes with dramatic suddenness. This self-acclaimed Deity on Christ's part demanded, in their view, His immediate death by stoning, according to the Law. Had His claim been unintentional He could easily have protested and explained. Instead, He simply "went forth out of their hand."

Again, He declares that when He, the Son of Man, ascends to Heaven, He will be "where He was before" (John 6. 62). Often did He say that He came forth from the Father, and that the Father had sent Him into the world; and in His closing prayer He places His pre-existence prior to creation, stating of His past glory that it was His with the Father "before the world was" (John 17. 5). **The Personal Word.**

It is in the light of these statements of the Lord Himself that we find an explanation of the opening words of the Gospel of John. Only in the sense of His eternal and Personal pre-existence can we rightly understand the declaration, "In the beginning was the Word." However the phrase "In the beginning" may be taken, whatsoever time our finite mind may conceive of, He who is the Word then "was." The statement does not predicate that He had beginning, that at any time He began to be, it says that in the beginning He was already existent, implying that He was unoriginated.

This passage, like others that have been mentioned, associates the past eternity of His Being with His Incarnation. "The Word was with God, and the Word was God...and the Word became flesh, and dwelt among us" (John 1. 1, 2, 14). There is not the slightest suggestion here that "The Word" was an abstract, impersonal quality. The whole passage cries out against the idea. This Gospel itself is a witness against it. He who is here called "The Word," who was "with God" and "was God," in union and yet distinction in the Godhead, is at the same time spoken of as the Creator. "All things were made by Him" (v. 3). In a similar manner the passage speaks of Him as "the Light," not an impersonal emanation, but a Being, who, as the Light, came into the world (v. 9, R.V.), and again in this respect, He is spoken of as the Creator: "the world was made by Him" (v. 10). He called Himself "the Light of the World." Personal as the Light, He was likewise personal as the Word. And then, further to emphasize His personality, the Apostle shows that He who is "the Word" is none other than the only begotten Son of God

(v. 18). This title, "only begotten," we must consider later. The identification of the Word with the Son is of itself sufficient to refute any idea that the Word, or Logos, ever was anything but a personal Being. His pre-existence, then, must have been co-eternal with that of the Father.

The Testimony of the Epistles.

The Epistles are likewise explicit as to this. The Apostle John, in his first Epistle, speaks of Christ as "the Word of Life...the eternal life, which was with the Father, and was manifested unto us" (1 John 1. 1, 2). In the Epistle to the Colossians, Paul says, "He is before all things, and in Him all things consist" (Col. 1. 17). There is therefore nothing that does not owe its existence to Him, nor anything that exists independently of Him. Again, in the introduction of the Epistle to the Hebrews, Christ is presented in His pre-existence as the Creator and as the Sustainer of all things, as the Sin-Purger at Calvary (Heb. 1. 3), and as the unchanging, ever lasting One in the future (v. 12). This passage associates the three, the eternal past, the central point of time, and the eternal future. The past eternity and the future eternity of His Being find their focus at the Cross.

And of Christ in the Apocalypse.

In the closing book He speaks from the glory, declaring three times that He is "The First, and the Last, and the Living One," the One who was dead and is "alive for evermore" (Rev. 1. 17, 18; 2. 8; 22. 13). His title, "the First," does not imply that He had a beginning, any more than "the Last" implies that He will have an end. These terms could not possibly signify that He belongs to the order of created beings. On the contrary, they are the terms which three times in Isaiah Jehovah uses of Himself (Isa. 41. 4; 44. 6; 48. 12). They therefore declare, in respect of the Son, what is true of the Father, His unoriginated and unending self-existence, His Divine power as the originating Cause of all creation, and His absolute supremacy over all.

The testimony of the Scriptures we have been considering as to Christ's pre-existence constitutes at the same time a witness to His essential Deity. That His goings forth were "from everlasting" could not be said of a created being. The prologue to John's Gospel not only shows that He was personally the Word, but definitely states that He was God (chap. 1. 1), and since He Himself declares that He came forth from the Father, and that He and the Father are One, He must have been eternally one with the Father in the Godhead. Again, both this Gospel and the Epistles state that He was the Creator of all things, a power which belongs alone to Deity.

As we contemplate the essential and eternal

The Pre-Existent One.

glory of Christ in the past eternity, we thereby learn to value more intelligently and adoringly His redemptive work on the Cross. May we thus be helped to take the low place at His feet, and, responding to God's grace in Him, worship and serve in fear and filial love all our days!

Lord Jesus Christ, Eternal Word,
  The Father's well-belovèd Son,
Thyself Creation's Source and Lord,
  Thou living, life-imparting One,
For life and pardon through Thy Blood
We praise Thy Name, O Son of God.

Thou Who from glory didst descend,
  The Father's glory, yet Thine own,
To shameful death Thy way to wend,
  That we might share Thy glorious Throne,
For 'grace abounding' through Thy Blood
We praise Thy Name, O Son of God.

Thou uncreated Life and Light,
  By Whom the heavens and earth were made,
On Calvary's tree, in death's dark night,
  By Thee our ransom price was paid.
For our redemption through Thy Blood
We praise Thy Name, O Son of God.

Exalted high at God's right hand,
  For Thy redeemed Thou soon wilt come,
Fulfilling all that grace has planned,
  Thy Father's House our destined home.
And all we owe to Thy shed Blood!
Blest be Thy Name, Thou Son of God.

CHAPTER II.

The Eternal Sonship of Christ.

THE subject of our opening chapter was the eternal pre-existence of Christ. The question now before us is whether in His pre-existence He was the Son of God, or whether He became so at His Incarnation. Many Scriptures which testify to His Divine Sonship might, apart from passages to the contrary, be regarded as suggesting (and have been so understood) that He became the Son of God at His birth, and that this title applies to Him only from that time onward. Should we find, however, that there are Scriptures which demonstrate His eternal Sonship in the past, we must understand the other passages in this light.

In the Epistle to the Galatians the Apostle states that "When the fulness of time came, **God Sent forth His Son,** born of a woman, born under the Law" (Gal. 4. 4). The reference plainly is to His being sent forth from Heaven to earth by incarnation, and not to any subsequent mission in the days of His flesh. This passage clearly indicates that God sent forth One who was already His Son. We may not read it as if it meant that "God sent forth One who in His birth became His Son," any more than the parallel statement in verse 6, "God sent forth the Spirit of His Son" (R.V.), could be taken to mean that God sent forth One who became His Spirit at the sending. The Spirit of God, sent forth at Pentecost, had ever been His Spirit. Similarly, verse 4 implies that He whom God sent forth was already His Son.

The Lord's Testimony.

With this agree the Lord's own statements recorded in the Gospel of John. He says to the disciples: "Ye...have believed that I came forth from the Father. I came out from the Father, and am come into the world; again, I leave the world, and go unto the Father" (John 16. 27, 28). In this He gives a plain intimation of His pre-existent relationship as the Son prior to the Incarnation. Some have considered His statement, "I came out from the Father," as pointing to an eternal procession from the Father in the past, or what has been termed the "eternal generation" of the Son. This, however, does not seem to be the Lord's meaning here. His statement, "Again, I leave the world and go unto the Father," expresses the reversal of His procedure mentioned in the first part of the verse. His going unto the Father is the antithesis of His coming out from the Father. What the Lord is teaching in this passage is not the inter-relations of Deity in the abstract, but His mission from the Father as having been sent by Him into the world.*

His words to the disciples are to be compared with His previous utterance to the Jews, "I came forth and am come from God; for neither have I come of Myself, but He sent Me." Here again the reference is plainly to His mission, and not to His Person.

The Testimony of John's First Epistle.

The Apostle John, in the introduction to his first Epistle, says, "The Life was manifested and we have seen, and bear witness, and declare unto you the Life, the Eternal Life, which was with the Father, and was manifested unto us" (1 John 1. 2). He does not here say that He who was the Life was "with God," but that He was "with the Father." The term "Father" implies the existence of a Son. The terms "father" and "son" are correlative. In no other sense than that of pre-existent Fatherhood and Sonship can the Apostle have made such a statement.

There is no hint in the Scriptures of any time

---

*It is true that the preposition *para* is used at the end of verse 27, while a different preposition *ek* is used in verse 28. We may not, however, press the meaning of *ek* as being "out of," and as denoting eternal generation. It states still more strongly than in the preceding clause His coming forth from Heaven to earth. Indeed, the Lord may here be emphasizing the fullness of His self-sacrificing love in leaving the glory to come into the world.

at which God began to be a Father; yet the above Scriptures make clear that His Fatherhood in relation to Christ was pre-existent to the Incarnation. The Fatherhood of the One being eternal, the Sonship of the Other must likewise have been eternal. In the light of this introductory statement in the Epistle, we are to understand the subsequent statement in chapter 4. 14, "The Father hath sent the Son to be the Saviour of the world." It was a Father who sent and a Son who came.

His Only Begotten Son.

These Scriptures provide us with the interpretation of other passages. When we read, for instance, that "God so loved the world, that He gave His only begotten Son" (John 3. 16), the statement may not be taken to mean that Christ became His only begotten Son by incarnation. That would rob the verse of its meaning and force. The value and greatness of the gift lay in the Sonship of Him who was given. His Sonship was not the effect of His being given.

The expression, "only begotten," which, as used of Christ, is found only in John's Gospel and his first Epistle, does not refer to His Incarnation. In the Gospel he says, "We beheld His glory, glory as of the (lit., an) only begotten from the (lit., a) Father" (1. 14)—not as in the Authorized Version, "*of* the Father." "From" rightly translates the word *para*; the same preposition is used in His words in chapter 7. 29, "I am from Him, and He sent Me." The glory was that of a Father's only begotten, the sole representative and manifestation of the being and character of the One who sent Him in virtue of the relationship. In other words, the glory to which John refers was the outshining of a unique, eternal, only begotten Sonship. In this relationship He came from Heaven to earth on His Father's mission.

In that same eternal sense we are to understand the statements that "the only begotten Son...is in the bosom of the Father" (chap. 1. 18), and that of chapter 3. 16 already quoted (cp. chap. 3. 18). This is made clear from what the Apostle says in his first Epistle, that "God hath sent His only begotten Son into the world, that we might live through Him" (1 John 4. 9). The sending was by way of His Incarnation, and not subsequent to it. That He is "the only begotten Son, which is in the bosom of the Father," expresses both His eternal union with the Father in the Godhead, and the ineffable intimacy and love between Them, the Son sharing all the Father's counsels and enjoying all His affections. The form of expression used in the original, and rendered "which is," indicates that "the bosom of the Father ever has been and ever will be the Son's dwelling place.

Only then in the sense of unoriginated relationship are we to understand the term "only begotten" when used of the Son. The word "Son," in the case of the Son of God, speaks of Him as the perfect archetype of all that the word connotes, whether in human relation or Divine; the expression, "only begotten," tells of the uniqueness of that relation in His case.

The Term, "Begotten."

That the word "begotten" should be used of the Son's relationship to the Father does not imply any beginning to His Sonship. It suggests relationship indeed, but must be distinguished from generation as applied to man. To endeavour to shape our ideas of Divine relationship according to our knowledge of human relationships is simply to betray our ignorance. The finite mind cannot conceive of that which is infinite. Our limitations of time and sense forbid our full apprehension of the eternal. Yet God has conveyed the facts relating to Himself in language the phraseology of which we can understand, though the facts themselves lie outside the range of human conception.

The Father's utterance, predictively recorded in Psalm 2. 7: "Thou art My Son; this day have I begotten Thee," and quoted in Acts 15. 33; Heb. 1. 5; and 5. 5, is to be distinguished from those passages which we have been considering, which speak of Christ as the Only Begotten. This latter signifies, as we have seen, an eternally pre-existing relationship; the utterance in Psalm 2 and its quotations point to a distinctive occasion, whether the Incarnation or the Resurrection.

The Term "Firstborn."

Again, the title "Firstborn" (Col. 1. 15, 18; Rom. 8. 29; Heb. 1. 6; Rev. 1. 5), as used of Christ, does not imply a beginning of His being, nor does it class Him with His creatures; it indicates the dignity of His pre-eminence over them. When, for instance, the Apostle Paul speaks of Him as "the Firstborn of all creation" (Col. 1. 15), the mode of expression in the original and the context of the passage, sufficiently guard against the idea that Christ is to be classed with the creation itself. The idiomatic form of expression distinguishes Him from all created beings, and declares His priority and superiority to them. The next verse is explanatory of this title, and shows that instead of being created, He was Himself the Creator. The term, "only begotten," is absolute; as such, Christ stands alone in timeless relationship with the Father. The term "firstborn" is relative; it does distinguish Him from all creatures, but it brings them in view so as to show His infinite superiority to them.

Human Recognition of His Sonship.

In the days of His earthly ministry the recognition of His Divine relationship as the Son of God, in whatever connection the title was used, was not based upon a recollection of His superhuman birth, but upon the exhibition of His Divine attributes; for even in His Manhood while on earth these were always His, even though they might not always be in exercise. For instance, Nathaniel's confession, "Rabbi, Thou art the Son of God" (John 1. 49), drawn from him by the display of the Lord's omniscience, was contingent, not upon Nathanael's possible acquaintance with the fact of the Divine character of Christ's birth, but upon a recognition of His Divine personality. Still more suggestive is Martha's confession, the result of the evidences of His Divine attributes, "I have believed that Thou art the Christ, the Son of God, even He that cometh into the world" (John 11. 27), a recognition at once of His preexistence as well as His Divine Sonship. The same is true of the effects of His omnipotence in stilling the storm, when the disciples worshipped Him, saying, "Of a truth Thou art the Son of God" (Matt. 14. 33). Such is the case also with the testimony of those who were possessed of demons, who, at the putting forth of His power to deliver the victims of this thraldom, cried out, "Thou art the Son of God" (Luke 4. 41). What

Christ had been in the past eternity was now known among men.

The Son Prior to Creation.

The writer of the Hebrews Epistle states that the words of Psalm 102. 25, "Of old hast Thou laid the foundations of the earth, and the heavens are the works of Thy hands; they shall perish, but Thou shalt endure," were addressed by the Father to the Son. That is to say, the utterance was spoken to the Son as such, long prior to His Incarnation. He was, then, already the Son when He created the heavens and the earth (Heb. 1. 8, 10). This makes clear the meaning of verse 2. It is "in a Son" that God has spoken to us. The omission of the definite article or pronoun serves to emphasize the relationship. It is true that He has spoken to us through a Son incarnate, but it is also through Him that "He made the worlds," proving that His Sonship did not begin in His Incarnation.

Again, the Epistle to the Hebrews states that the brief biography of Melchizedek in Genesis was so shaped that, by the omission of his parentage and his death, he was made (*i.e.*, in the inspired narrative) "like unto the Son of God," and the similarity lay in this, that he had "neither beginning of days nor end of life." Accordingly it was as the Son of God that Christ was without beginning of days. His Sonship was therefore unoriginated and eternal.

"He that Confesseth the Son."

Disbelief in the eternal pre-existent Sonship of Christ, while acknowledging God as everlasting Father, is transgression of His express word, that all should "honour the Son even as they honour the Father" (John 5. 23). To deny the eternity of the Son while admitting it in the case of the Father, cannot be ascribing equal honour to Them. "Whoso denieth the Son, the same hath not the Father: he that confesseth the Son hath the Father also." Let us see to it that we abide in the truth, that we may "abide in the Son and in the Father" (1 John 2. 23, 24). Only as we rightly consider the excellences of His eternal glory as the Son of God can our hearts be bowed in due adoration of Him who stooped to the Death of the Cross in order to bring us nigh to God.

CHAPTER III.

The Incarnation of Our Lord.

WHAT is said of the meal offering in the second and sixth chapters of Leviticus reminds us that the Incarnation can only rightly be considered in the Holy Place, and that it is a subject of meditation for those alone who are in the relationship of priests to God. As we ponder it let us worship and adore.

"When the fullness of the time came, God sent forth His Son, born of a woman, born under the Law" (Gal. 4. 4). "Born of a woman!" A special significance attaches to this. The Apostle hereby distinguishes the birth of Christ from that of all others. Were it not so he would just be stating a fact of common experience and wasting his words on a mere superfluity of detail. That is not Paul's way. His argument has no room for a simple truism. No one, in writing a biographical sketch of an ordinary man, would think of saying he was born of a woman. No! For the Apostle thus to speak of Christ is both to distinguish Him in accordance with His Divine and pre-existent Sonship as just set forth by him, and at the same time to testify both to His real humanity and His supernatural birth

The Incarnation of Our Lord.

"The Word Became Flesh."

This statement of the Incarnation of Christ is in the closest agreement with other passages of Scripture relating to the subject. The word rendered "born" is not *gennaō*, the ordinary word to describe "birth", but *ginomai*, "to become", and this is the word used in the declaration in John 1. 14, "the Word became flesh", and again in Philippians 2. 7, "becoming in the likeness of men" (R. V., *margin*). In the former passage, as we have previously observed, "the Word" is not an impersonal *Logos*, but "the only begotten Son of God." So the opening of the Gospel identifies Him. He Whom God sent forth was His Son. God did not send Him forth into the body of a man. He "was manifested in the flesh" (1 Tim. 3. 16). He became flesh, possessing full and perfect manhood, body, soul and spirit. These three constitute the totality of all that is essential to manhood, and this is here the meaning of the word "flesh". Christ Himself speaks of His body and of His soul, and of His spirit. Of the emblematic significance of the loaf in the Lord's Supper He said, "This is My *body.*" In the dark hour of Gethsemane He said, "My *soul* is exceeding sorrowful." And on the cross, "Father, into Thy hands I commit My *spirit.*" He did not come into flesh, He became flesh, and what He became He is now and ever will be, for He is coming in flesh (2 John 7), which plainly refers to the Second Advent.

The Reality of His Manhood
is expressed also in the Philippians passage referred to above. Christ Jesus, "being in the form of God, counted it not a thing to be grasped (or a means of self-aggrandizement) to be on an equality with God, but emptied Himself, taking the form of a servant, becoming in the likeness of men" (see *margin*). There is fuller reference to this passage later, when we consider the Servant-character of Christ. His becoming in the likeness of men explains how He took the form of a servant. The expression "likeness of men" in no way negatives the reality of His Manhood. The Apostle does not say "the likeness of a man," but "the likeness of men," *i.e.*, as they actually are—a mode of existence new to Him. Only of One who was more than man could this be predicated. True Manhood was His, and not a mere resemblance thereto. In becoming—what He was not before—man, He did not cease to be what He ever had been—God.

The Incarnation of Christ was

Not the Union of Two Persons,
one Divine and the other human. The seat of His Personality was His ever existing Deity. He said, "Before Abraham was I am," and "He that hath seen Me hath seen the Father." His Manhood

was not at any time independently personal. In our case the seat of personality is found in the human spirit, but the Man Christ Jesus was identical in Person with the Eternal Word. In Him there was no personal subsistence but one, and that from everlasting. By taking manhood He still continues and remains one and the same Person, changing only the manner of His subsisting. He who before was in the nature of the Son of God alone, became also, and now is, in the nature of man. Hence we prefer to say that He became "man" and not "a man." If He were not the same Person, the Son of God, who, being in the form of God, took the form of a bond-servant and became obedient even to the death of the Cross, then the whole point of the passage in Philippians, namely His grace in thus acting, would be lost.

It is of Christ Himself that everything is predicated, and not of His Divine nature on the one hand and of His human nature on the other. He acted Personally, not by this or that nature, but as One in the unity of whose Person the two natures are inseparably combined, "without confusion or conversion," as against the Eutychians, who supposed that the Humanity of Christ was absorbed into His Deity, and "without division, without separation," as against the Nestorians, who divided and separated the natures. It is the same Being who acts all through.

Nor, again, did either the Father or the Spirit become incarnate, as the Patripassians taught. Manhood is predicated only of the Son. "In Him dwelleth all the fullness of the Godhead bodily" (Col. 2. 9).

The two questions now arise:

How was the Incarnation Possible?

and, How was it accomplished? The first receives an answer at the beginning of the Old Testament, the second at the beginning of the New. "God created man in His own image" (Gen. 1. 27). Man marred the Divine handiwork by his self-will. That was the effect of the Fall. The narrative which describes it records the Divine plan for the recovery of the guilty and the restoration of the broken harmony of man's being The Lord God Himself uttered the initial prophecy of the Incarnation. It was the Seed of the woman who would bruise the serpent's head (Gen. 3. 15). The apprehension of this led Adam to call his wife's name Eve, "the living one." The giving of that name was faith's response to the Divine promise. "Living," not because her own life was spared, but because of her motherhood (v. 20). Life by means of the seed of the woman, that is the message latent in the name of the mother of mankind.

How was the Incarnation Accomplished?

As to the second question—how the Incarnation

became an accomplished fact, the sanctity of the theme demands the reverence of unshod feet. Speculation is banned. The Gospel narratives with their unencumbered statement of fact provide all that is necessary for faith. Matthew's Gospel records the Divine message to Joseph, given him in a dream: "Joseph, thou son of David, fear not to take unto thee Mary thy wife: for that which is conceived in her is of the Holy Ghost. And she shall bring forth a Son; and thou shalt call His Name Jesus; for it is He that shall save His people from their sins. Now all this is come to pass, that it might be fulfilled which was spoken by the Lord through the prophet, saying, Behold, the virgin shall be with child, and shall bring forth a Son, and they shall call His Name Immanuel" (Matt. 1. 20-23, R.V.).

Luke's Gospel records the message given to the Virgin Mary personally by the angel Gabriel. Replying to her inquiry how the promise of a Son could be fulfilled in her unmarried state, he said, "The Holy Ghost shall come upon thee, and the power of the Most High shall overshadow thee: wherefore the holy thing which is to be born shall be called the Son of God" (*marginal rendering*).

The faith of betrothed Joseph and Mary was remarkable. The naturally troubled state of Joseph's mind at finding that Mary was with child before they came together is intimated by

Matthew (chap. 1. 20). That, notwithstanding, he took Mary to wife, was the obedience of faith. Still more striking was the faith of Mary herself, when in her response to the Divine communication she said, "Behold, the handmaid (rather, "the bondmaid," *doulē*) of the Lord; be it unto me according to Thy word." Mere human considerations might have led her at least to refrain from such a ready acceptance of a situation which would naturally be misunderstood by people and be made a matter of idle talk.

By the overshadowing power of the Most High, and through the Holy Spirit, the Son of God became Incarnate, partaking with us in blood and flesh, the Creator Himself becoming part of the very creation He had called into existence (Heb. 2. 14). The Christ was truly "born" of the woman. The language of Scripture precludes the ancient Monophysite (one nature) theory, that He did not partake of her substance, a denial, in other words, that He became incarnate through His mother.

The truth of the Virgin Birth of Christ is
Essential to the Christian Faith,
it stands in inseparable connection with His acknowledged sinlessness and with the other evidences of the supernatural character of His Person. The Gospel narratives of His acts and His teaching banish all incongruity from the

initial and preliminary statements of His supernatural birth. His own claims as the Son of God would be invalidated if He were not of the Virgin born. Accept as facts the records of His life, and the unbiassed reader is compelled to accept the statements of His Virgin Birth. Deny the latter, and doubts must be entertained as to the character and attributes of the Person who stands before us in the Gospel narratives. Disbelief in the Virgin Birth and professed acceptance of the remainder of the records concerning Him are entirely inconsistent.

The accounts of the Birth of Christ in the Gospels of Matthew and Luke are undeniably genuine parts of these Gospels respectively. The chapters giving the record of the nativity are found in all the manuscripts. In each Gospel the first chapters come to us on precisely the same authority as the remaining chapters. The genuineness of these writings has been fully vindicated. The internal evidences are sufficient to show that the story of the Virgin Birth of Christ could never have been invented.

It is argued that the Virgin Birth of Christ does not help to explain His sinlessness and that the taint of sin might have been conveyed by Mary, since hers was a sinful nature. The argument is groundless, however. The overshadowing of the Most High, the power of the Holy Spirit, and the act of the Son of God Himself in the Incarnation, were sufficient to secure absolute freedom from taint of sin. As we have remarked above, the Birth of Christ was not the generation of a new Being. It was the entrance, on the part of One who was already God, upon a new mode of existence, and hence "the Holy One" remained holy.

"The Grace of our Lord Jesus Christ."
"Ye know the grace," says the Apostle, "of our Lord Jesus Christ, that though He was rich, yet for your sakes He became poor, that ye through His poverty might become rich." This is the meaning and message of the Incarnation. It is not a matter of cold theology. Never can we rightly contemplate the theme without the stirring of our deepest gratitude and affection. Nay, more, be it ours, constrained by such wondrous grace, to render to Him in loving devotion "all we have and are."

> "He has come! the Christ of God
> Left for us His glad abode,
> Stooping from His throne of bliss
> To this darksome wilderness.
>
> "He the Mighty King has come!
> Making this poor earth His home;
> Come to bear our sins' sad load,
> Son of David, Son of God.
>
> "Unto us a Son is given!
> He has come from God's own Heaven,
> Bringing with Him from above
> Holy peace and holy love." H. BONAR.

CHAPTER IV

The Perfect Servant.

THE purposes for which Christ Jesus came into the world are variously stated in Scripture. He came "to seek and to save that which was lost" (Luke 19. 10). He came to call sinners to repentance (chap. 5. 32), and to save them (1 Tim. 1. 15). His primary object, however, was to do the will of His Father. "I am come down from Heaven," He says, "not to do Mine own will, but the will of Him that sent Me" (John 6. 38). This was His very sustenance, His "meat" (chap. 4. 34). He alone could say absolutely, "I delight to do Thy will, O My God: yea, Thy Law is within My heart" (Psa. 40. 8).

His path of undeviating obedience to the Father marked Him as the One of Whom Jehovah had said through the prophet Isaiah, "Behold My Servant, Whom I uphold; My chosen, in Whom My soul delighteth" (Isa. 42. 1). "Who, being* in

---

*Or rather, "existing;" the word *huparchō* carries with it a twofold idea, firstly, that what is predicated of this Person characterized Him in a special manner both before and at the time referred to, and, secondly, that He continued so to be characterized after the particular event stated of Him. To take an illustration, "Joseph who was (*huparchōn*, being) a councillor . . . went to Pilate, and asked for the body of Jesus" (Luke 23. 50, 52). He did not cease to be a councillor after his request from Pilate. So Christ did not cease to be "in the form of God" after becoming Man.

the form of God (not a resemblance to God, but that mode of being which reveals the essential nature and character of God†) counted it not a prize (more accurately as in the margin), "a thing to be grasped" (the true meaning probably is 'a means of self-aggrandisement') to be on an equality with God, but emptied Himself, taking the form of a servant, being made (lit. becoming) in the likeness of men" (Phil. 2. 6, 7).

A Bondservant.

He took the form of a "bondservant." This He never was said to be in relation to men, for the word implies the complete yielding of the will to the one served. He was indeed the servant (*diakonos*) of men; so He spoke of Himself, for instance, when, correcting the ambitious rivalry of the disciples, He said, "Whosoever would become great among you shall be your minister (*diakonos*): and whosoever would be first among you, shall be servant of all. For verily the Son of Man came not to be ministered unto, but to minister, and to give His life a ransom for many" (Mark 10. 43-45). So again in the upper room, setting Himself in contrast to their questioning as to which of them was the greatest, He says, "I am in the midst of you as

---

†That is the meaning of the word *morphè*, form; it denotes the manifestation of the reality inseparable from the person or thing mentioned.

He that serveth" (Luke 22. 27). *Diakonos* implies activity in ministry directed by one's own judgment, while *doulos* implies subjection to the will of another, and hence the latter word is said of Christ solely in relation to His service to Him who sent Him. He was the *diakonos* of men, the *doulos* of God. Precisely as the phrase, "the form of a servant," expresses the reality and the character of His position as a Servant, for that He undeniably was, so "the form of God" expresses the reality of His Deity. He was as truly God, both in His pre-existence and subsequently after becoming Incarnate, as He was a Servant when on earth.

His Divine Attributes.

Since the phrases, "taking the form of a servant, becoming in the likeness of men" (Phil. 2. 7), explain the preceding statement that "He emptied Himself," it is important to observe carefully the testimony of the Gospel narratives concerning His attributes and ways as Jehovah's Servant. That He remained in the fullest sense God, is, as we have seen, made clear throughout this passage. It is also directly stated in several places in the New Testament. The Gospels present Him as One Who, while possessed of the Divine attributes, exercised these in dependence on, and subjection to, the Father. The power He displayed was that which belongs only to God.

Nature was completely subject to His control. He walked on the water, He stilled the tempest with a word, He turned water into wine, He supernaturally provided bread. Again, He had absolute power over disease and death; He healed "all manner of disease and all manner of sickness" (Matt. 4. 23), and He raised the dead. A single utterance from His lips caused His would-be captors to fall backward to the ground (John 18. 6).*

Again, "He knew all men," "He knew what was in man" (John 2. 24, 25). He knew the secret history of people's lives (chap. 4. 16-19), and their destiny (chaps. 5. 24-29; 8. 21). He perceived men's thoughts (Mark 2. 8; Luke 5. 22). He displayed a knowledge of the future impossible to men. His forecast of future events has so far been fulfilled with absolute precision.†

---

*The miracles of Christ are to be distinguished from those wrought by Apostles, prophets, and others. In their case a miracle was accomplished by Divinely imparted power. Compare Peter's statement as to the healing of the lame man, "Why marvel ye at this man? Or why fasten your eyes on us, as though by our own power or godliness we had made him to walk?" (Acts. 3. 12). Christ was Himself One in the Godhead and, therefore, had all the attributes of Deity, while, being also Man, He acted in the power of the Spirit.

†In this connection we may notice what the Lord says about His knowledge of the Father. In one of the discussions with the opposing Jews He says, "Ye have not known Him; but I know Him" (John 8. 55). In the former statement the word is *ginoskō*, indicating knowledge derived from experience; in the latter it is *oida*, signifying intuitive knowledge. He thus differentiates Himself entirely from the Jews. It is true that He uses the word *ginoskō* of His knowledge of the Father, as He does also of the Father's knowledge of Himself, as, for instance, in John 10. 15, where He says, "Even as the Father knoweth Me, and I know the Father."

The Perfect Servant. 31

Deeply significant, too, is the fact that the Lord could see what was going on, though in bodily presence He was not there to behold it. He says to Nathaniel, "Before Philip called thee, when thou wast under the fig tree, I saw thee" (John 1. 48). It was nothing but the evidence of Christ's Divinely supernatural powers that drew from Nathaniel the exclamation, "Rabbi, Thou art the Son of God; Thou art King of Israel." And the Lord admitted the evidence of His Deity by His recognition of the man's faith; He says, "Because I said unto thee, I saw thee underneath the fig tree, believest thou? Thou shalt see greater things than these."

His Obedience to the Father.

Now the passage in Philippians 2, which shows that Deity was still His in and after His Incarnation, likewise states that He became "obedient even unto death." His whole life was one of undeviating obedience to the Father, and His death was the culminating act thereof. "He learned obedience (it does not say that He learned to obey) by the things which He suffered" (Heb. 5. 8). He never did anything independently of the Father. He said, "The Son can do nothing of (lit. from) Himself, but what He seeth the Father doing" (John 5. 19). This did not signify intrinsic limitations in His case; His limitations were only such as He voluntarily imposed upon Himself. For, He further says, "for what things soever He doeth, these the Son also doeth in like manner." All that He did was done in inseparable union with the Father. He said, "I and the Father are One," and again, "My Father worketh even until now, and I work." Supernatural power, therefore, inalienably belonged to Him as the Son. Yet He ever acted as One Who in virtue of His Manhood was dependent on, and in subjection to, the will of His Father.

His Anointing.

Again, He declared that He wrought signs by the Spirit of God (Matt. 12. 28). The Apostle Peter also, referring to the time of Christ's baptism in the Jordan, states that "God anointed Him with the Holy Ghost and with power" (Acts 10. 38). This does not imply that Christ was in Himself void of supernatural power, or not possessed of the attributes of Godhead prior to His being so anointed, nor does it imply that He was without the Holy Spirit up to that time. His works were wrought as a result of a Divine unction. And herein we learn more fully the glory of His grace as the Perfect Servant; for it shows that, while His Deity gives to all He did a unique character and value, He did not act merely in virtue of His Godhood, but, continuing the position of dependence on, and subjection to, the Father, He lived and taught and wrought and offered up Himself, and won His mighty victory, in the power of the Spirit. Had it not been so He would have failed to preserve perfectly the place of a bondservant, which He took so really in this world.

He Laid Down His Life.

In His "becoming in the likeness of men," His Body itself became the instrument of His fulfilment of the Father's will. This Psalm 40 foretold, as quoted in Hebrews. "When He cometh into the world, He saith, Sacrifice and offering thou wouldest not, but a body didst Thou prepare for Me: in burnt offerings and sacrifices for sin Thou hast had no pleasure. Then said I, Lo, I am come (in the roll of the book it is written of Me), to do Thy will, O God" (Heb. 10. 5-7. He could and did restrict the use of His Divine attributes. He allowed His captors to bind Him after the display of His Divine power in prostrating them with His word. He subjected Himself to human violence and indignity. He permitted those who had charge of His Crucifixion to carry out their deed. "He was crucified through weakness" (2 Cor. 13. 4), not through helplessness, nor through weakness caused by maltreatment, but by the voluntary suspension of His essential power as the Son of God. Human force itself was absolutely unavailing against

Him save as it was His will to submit thereto. In proof whereof He said of Himself, what could not possibly be true of any mere man, "I lay down My life, that I may take it again. No one taketh it away from Me, but I lay it down of Myself. I have power (or authority) to lay it down, and I have power to take it again. This commandment received I from My Father" (John 10. 17, 18).

The restrictions He imposed on Himself are consistent with His true Manhood. At the same time in these very restrictions He constantly displayed His supernatural power. Nowhere is this more strikingly exhibited than on the Cross. Certain details regarding His Death distinguish it from the crucifixion of a mere man, as, for example, His mighty shout, the dismissal of His spirit, and prior to it the bowing (or rather, reclining) of His head, in contrast to the natural order in which the last breath is followed by the drooping of the head. His death could not have been the death of a mere man. It is useless to argue that God cannot die and therefore Christ was not God. He who was God could become also Man in order to die, and this He did. His death was the supernatural death of One who was both Man and God.

"Of That Day And That Hour."

As with His Divine power, so with His Divine knowledge, referring to His Second Advent He said, "But of that day or that hour knoweth no one, not even the angels in Heaven, neither the Son, but the Father" (Mark 13. 22). This was not failure in knowledge. Indeed, it is quite possible that the original conveys the thought that the Son's knowledge is only in conjunction with the Father's. This would be in keeping with His statements, "My judgment is true; for I am not alone, but I and the Father that sent Me" (John 8. 16); "I speak that which I have seen with My Father" (5. 38). The Lord's statement in Mark 13 is proof that He possessed powers of knowledge which belong to God alone. It likewise displays His character as the perfect Servant of Jehovah. John 11. 17-34 is another instance of this. It was in the path of the Father's will that after Lazarus's death, He waited two days before going, and on arriving inquired how long he had been buried and where. All this evinced His compassionate tenderness towards those who were in sorrow.

The Scriptures plainly teach, then, both that the Lord never abandoned His Divine attributes, and that He sat as a scholar in the Father's school and learned from Him His daily will. It was of Christ that Isaiah wrote, "The Lord God hath given me the tongue of them that are taught . . . He wakeneth morning by morning, He wakeneth mine ear to hear as they that are taught" (Isa. 50. 4, 5).

The Barren Fig Tree.

In the case of the fig tree recorded in Mark 11. 13, He decided to make use of the ordinary means of investigation common to men. "Seeing a fig tree afar off having leaves, He came if haply He might find anything thereon." Here the fig tree was fruitless. 'The season was not of figs.' The figs should have been there before the leaves if there was to be fruit at all. Immediately, and with a view to the moral significance of His act, He dooms the fig tree to destruction. Both in the investigation and in the destruction He fulfilled the Father's will in perfect communion with Him.

All such instances, while evidences of the true humanity of our Lord, are at the same time to be regarded in the light of His essential Deity. Not that the attributes of the Divine were communicated to the human nature; the Lord's acts were those of One Who was in the possession of both natures. He never acted at one time as man and at another as God. The two natures were, and are, perfectly and inseparately combined in Him. The restrictions He imposed upon Himself illustrate then the Apostle's statement that Christ "emptied Himself, taking the form of a servant." They reveal the essential reality of His Servant character, and only so can they be rightly considered. They are not matters of mere Christology.

His Example to Us.

We behold Him, therefore, as One who undeviatingly delighted to do the will of the Father, never permitting anything to mar the glory of His Filial service and obedience. This was His greatest joy, the joy that breathes through His statements, "I can of Myself do nothing; as I hear I judge: and My judgment is righteous; because I seek not Mine own will, but the will of Him that sent Me"*(John 5. 30).

So, again, when leaving the upper room with His disciples, with the horrors of Gethsemane, His betrayal, His trial, and death, before Him, He says, "I love the Father, and as the Father gave Me commandment even so I do"(chap. 14. 31). This was the spirit that found expression at the hour of His dark Gethsemane conflict, in His utterance of sublime resignation, "Father, if Thou be willing, remove this cup from Me: nevertheless not My will, but Thine be done."

May our contemplation of the Son of God ever lead our hearts to worship and adore Him, and, while we consider Him in the perfection of His ways, let us remember that He "left us an example that we should follow His steps." And let us find our delight in doing His will. For to us His word applies, "As the Father hath sent Me, even so send I you."

---
*See also John 4. 34; 5. 19, quoted before.

CHAPTER V.

The Sinlessness of Christ.

THE witness of the writers of the New Testament to the sinlessness of Christ is varied yet unanimous. And the witness is the more cogent in that neither the variety nor the unanimity can possibly have been prearranged. Even the most critical reader, be he candid, is compelled to admit the impossibility that the writers can have agreed to a consensus of opinion upon this subject. Indeed the very diversity of the testimony is against the idea.

We will take first the direct statements of the writers themselves. We might have expected to find assertions as to the sinlessness of Christ made by the writers of the Gospels. Their testimony, striking in itself, is however, of a different sort. It is true that certain of the characters in their writings make definite pronouncements, but for assertions on the part of those who wrote the New Testament we must turn to the Epistles. And here the testimony is strikingly appropriate to the character or circumstances respectively of those writers who predicate His sinlessness.

The Testimony of the Apostles.

The Apostle Peter's testimony is that He *did*

THE SINLESSNESS OF CHRIST.   39

no sin (1 Peter 2. 22). This comes appropriately from one who was characteristically a man quick to act. He adds, "neither was guile found in His mouth," perhaps with a recollection of his own waywardness of utterance on the night of His betrayal. John says, "*In Him is* no sin" (1 John 3. 5). The Gospels make clear that to this Apostle was granted a special nearness to, and intimacy with, the Lord in the days of His flesh, as, for instance, when at the Supper he leaned on Jesus' breast (John 13. 23-26). He, then, testifies, not to the outward acts, but to the inner being of the Lord.

A third form of testimony comes from Paul's pen, namely, that Christ "*knew* no sin" (2 Cor. 5. 21). This is peculiarly fitting on the part of one to whom it was committed to communicate so much of the Lord's mind, and who says, "we have the mind of Christ" (1 Cor. 2. 16), and later exhorts the saints to have the mind which was in Him (Phil. 2. 5).

The fullest statements are made by the writer of the Epistle to the Hebrews, and this is consistent with the fact that practically the whole Epistle is occupied with the glories of Christ. Here we read that He was "in all points tempted like as we are, yet *without sin*;" that He was "holy, guileless, undefiled, separated from sinners" (Heb. 4. 15; 7. 26).

The Witness of the Gospels.

We turn now from direct statements of this sort to the testimony of the Gospels. The Gospels provide a threefold witness; (1) that of the character and ways of Christ; (2) the utterances of Christ Himself; (3) the testimony of His adversaries.

His Character and Ways.

(1) The writers of the Gospels, as we have said, do not themselves state therein that Christ was sinless. How readily could they have done so! How easily they might have sounded His praises, discoursed on His perfections, or spoken with admiration of His flawless character! The absence of all such remarks makes their presentation the more striking. With unvarnished naturalness and simplicity they state facts seen by them or communicated to them, and the Person whom they each present, independently of one another indeed, and yet with perfect consistency, is seen to be the very archetype of holiness, whose stainless beauty and unsullied glory stamp with imperfection everything apart from Himself.

Christ did not become sinless, He was so from the beginning. He never gave a trace of strife against inward moral contradictions. The closest scrutiny can never detect the slightest degree of repentance or remorse on His part.

He never prayed for forgiveness, for He had no sin to confess. No sentence He ever uttered could be construed to indicate a consciousness of guilt, or an admission of unworthiness. In urging repentance upon men, it was for their own sins; He never identified Himself with them in this need. When overtaken by calamity men spontaneously admit their sinfulness. Never did Christ, in the hours of His greatest distress, betray in the least degree, in the outpourings of His soul, a consciousness of error.

Contact Without Contamination.

Nor again could it ever be said that His holiness was preserved by avoiding contact with defilement. He lived not the life of a recluse. He neither turned aside from conflict with the Tempter, nor did He avoid the company of the sinful. It was a taunt of His arch-critics that He was "the friend of publicans and sinners." The Gospels present Him as truly Man, a member of the human race, belonging as such to all races and all generations of mankind, identifying Himself with humanity in everything but sin. He is found continually in the closest contact with the degraded and defiled, surrounded constantly by a multitude of malignant influences, yet He remained absolutely untainted by their defilement. In this He was essentially distinct from even the holiest of ordinary men. Those who were nearest to Him in character were those who felt themselves at the greatest moral distance from Him.

Yet His was by no means a mechanical faultlessness; He was "tempted in all points like as we are." The question is often raised, how could temptation be real to Christ, considering His absolute sinlessness? The Scripture says that "He suffered being tempted," and that on this account it is that He is "able to succour them that are tempted" (Heb. 2. 18). He suffered being tempted! His very power to suffer and His moral perfection made the force of temptation the more real and terrible to Him. The trustworthy chain that stands the strain is as much tested as the untrustworthy chain that breaks. The greater the reliability the greater the test. It is the chain that cannot break that has the greatest testing. It is the one who never yields who feels the fullest force of a temptation and suffers the most.

His Own Claims.

(2) Christ Himself claims that He was sinless. With an incontestable challenge to His keenest adversaries, and a certainty that the challenge could not be accepted, He says, "which of you convicteth Me of sin?" (John 8. 46). To His disciples He says, "The prince of this world cometh: and he hath nothing in Me" (John 16. 30).

THE SINLESSNESS OF CHRIST. 43

There was nothing in Him which could respond to the suggestions or instigations of the Evil One.

It has been urged that when, to the ruler who inquired what he should do to inherit eternal life, the Lord said, "Why callest thou Me good? None is good save One, even God," He was disclaiming the title of good. Such a conclusion is due to a misunderstanding of the circumstances. The ruler used the word "good" with an inadequate perception of the meaning of the term; his use of it indicated a misapprehension of his own sinfulness. Christ intimated in His reply that if the term were to be applied to Him at all, it must be used in its highest sense, namely, as it is applicable to God. So far, therefore, from suggesting a consciousness of imperfection or failure on His part, the Lord was intimating the very reverse. The pedestal on which the young man placed Him was not really high enough (Matt. 19. 16-22).

Here, as in other instances, He showed Himself in conflict with the customary views of what was good. As has been said, "He came into violent collision with them, and with creative originality set forth, in His teaching, life and suffering, a view of the good directly opposed to the prevailing one," and that in a way "only possible if He Himself was possessed and filled by the glory of the truly and essentially good which He knew and brought to light," the good which was Divinely and intrinsically His own.

The Testimony of His Foes.

(3) The witness of His adversaries is varied, again, and yet concordant. Demons acknowledged Him as "the Holy One of God" (Mark 1. 24), an appellation applicable to none other save Christ Jesus; it predicates His absolute freedom from taint of sin. Negatively, His bitterest foes the Pharisees, assiduously watching through the whole course of His public ministry to find even the slightest fault in Him, plotting to catch Him in His words, prying frequently even into His private life, could at length raise no charge against Him but the baseless accusation of shewing disrespect to Cæsar, a charge declared void by the Roman judge who sat to hear the case.

His betrayer remorsefully said, "I have betrayed innocent blood."

His judge declared, "I find no fault in this Man"

His executioner exclaimed, "Certainly this was a righteous Man."

Did He Adapt His Teachings to Human Ignorance?

Under the weight of this threefold array of evidence the imputation falls to the ground that Christ, upon occasion in His teachings, adjusted His ideas to the ignorance of the people, or made use of Jewish myths to give instruction and

THE SINLESSNESS OF CHRIST. 45

warning; as when, for instance, He narrated the circumstances of the death and destinies of the rich man and Lazarus (Luke 16. 19-13). How gross a misconception to imagine that He, "in whose mouth there was no guile," concerning whom the testimony that He was "holy, guileless, undefiled" has been vindicated from every point of view, descended to adopt methods of deception! That He, whose heart was itself the very shrine of Divine holiness, who declared with unchallengeable authority that the judgment of all men had been committed to Him, ever trifled with men's ignorance, and that, too, in matters relating to human destiny in the other world! The imputation is an outrage upon His sacred Name.

In the life of every other man there is disharmony: the disintegrating effects of sin are universal to the human race. With Christ alone it is different. His nature is disclosed to us as that of the sublimest and purest harmony. Reason and will were never divorced in His case. Never with Him did any mental or moral faculty unduly preponderate. For example, He exhibited vitality of emotion and feeling, but never so that they passed into passionate excitement. All His ways were characterized by a sublime dignity. The unbroken harmony of His nature was in keeping with His unbroken harmony with the Father. In this, as to His Godhood,

His words apply, "I and the Father are One."

Inevitable Conclusions.

From the sinlessness of Christ certain considerations follow. His uniqueness in this respect involves the uniqueness of His Birth. Birth by natural generation has produced no exception among men to invalidate the pronouncement that "All have sinned, and fall short of the glory of God." Not so with Christ Jesus. His sinlessness vindicates the doctrine of His Virgin Birth, and explains the fact. Again, His sinless life gave Him a claim, by the Divine Law, to exemption from Death. Yet He died. His death must, therefore, have been vicarious. "Christ died for our sins." "He was wounded for our transgressions, He was bruised for our iniquities." Further, His sinlessness determined His resurrection as His rightful prerogative. God's Holy One could never see corruption. In His case "Death could not hold its prey." Hence to His perverted and arbitrary judges He declared, with the knowledge of the Death which lay before Him, that He would be raised to "the right hand of the power of God" and would appear in Divine glory and majesty.

The character of His life on earth shewed that He was perfectly fitted to undertake the work of redeeming grace in the atoning sacrifice on the Cross. We are redeemed "with precious Blood,

THE SINLESSNESS OF CHRIST. 47

as of a lamb without blemish and without spot, even the Blood of Christ" (1 Peter 1. 19). "Him who knew no sin, He made to be sin on our behalf; that we might become the righteousness of God in Him" (2 Cor. 5. 21).

"In His spotless soul's distress,
I perceive my guiltiness;
O how vile my low estate,
Since my ransom was so great."

CHAPTER VI.

The Moral Glories of Christ.

> "Join all the glorious names,
> Of wisdom, love, and power,
> That mortals ever knew,
> That angels ever bore;
> All are too mean to speak His worth,
> Too mean to set our Saviour forth."

THE perfections which mark the life and testimony of the Lord Jesus answer to the prophetic description of His character given by the Spirit through the Psalmist, "Thou art fairer than the children of men; grace is poured into Thy lips" (Psa. 45. 2). The full apprehension of His moral glories lies beyond human ken. For the first time the eyes of the Father rested upon One on earth with infinite satisfaction and appreciation. He grew up before Him "as a tender plant, and as a root out of a dry ground." From the earliest days of His life on earth, and at every stage of His growth into manhood, He gave that unmingled delight to the Father which found expression at His baptism in the voice out of the Heavens, saying, "This is My beloved Son, in Whom I am well pleased" (Matt. 3. 17).

The successive stages of His childhood and youth

The Moral Glories of Christ. 49

are briefly summed up in the statement in Luke's Gospel: "The child grew, and waxed strong, filled with wisdom: and the grace of God was upon Him," and "Jesus advanced in wisdom and stature, and in favour with God and men" (Luke 2. 40,52). Truly child, youth, man, He was at every stage possessed of the full orb of moral perfections, and that complete blending of those traits of character which marked Him as "the Holy One of God."

The Harmony of His Character.

The perfectly adjusted combination and correlation of virtues exhibited in His life, distinguish Him from all others. The greatest and best of men give evidence of some amount of unevenness in disposition, some preponderance of one trait of character over another. There was no such disproportion in the Lord Jesus. His character never received modification nor readjustment. It was the same throughout, possessing always the same even balance and harmony. In Him majesty was perfectly blended with meekness, dignity with condescension, conscious greatness with unostentatious simplicity, power with mercy, justice with benevolence, holy indignation against sin with tender compassion for the sinner. His gentleness was never characterized by weakness, nor His love by mere sentimentality. His zeal never degenerated into impulsiveness, nor His calmness into indifference. The complete constellation of virtues shone in His character with undimmed lustre, irradiating all His utterances and ways, and imparting an unexampled unity to His different actions. No situation, however critical, found Him at variance with Himself. "Grace and truth came by Jesus Christ." His untiring interest in the welfare of man was at the same time characterized by undeviating devotion to the Father.

The Initial Gospel Records.

The glories of His character, which are so considerably veiled from us as regards His early years in the home at Nazareth, shine forth in all their beauty immediately the Gospel records begin to depict His public life and testimony. One's first thought is to speak of those deeds of grace and truth in the marriage feast at Cana of Galilee and the cleansing of the temple. But on considering these as following upon His temptation in the wilderness a striking connection becomes evident. How much is lost by failure to compare the various Gospel narratives one with another! Not merely with reference to the same incidents recorded in them, but in the arrangement of the order of different incidents! Quite recently it occurred to the writer that there might be a certain correspondence between the moral glories of the Lord in the circumstances of

THE MORAL GLORIES OF CHRIST. 51

His threefold temptation by Satan, as recorded in the earlier Gospels, and the character of His first public acts and teachings as narrated by John. A comparison at once revealed coincidences obviously designed by the Spirit of God, and possibly present also to the mind of John. The correspondence is with the order of the temptations as given in Matthew's Gospel. That order is chronological. Where Luke's order differs from that of the other Gospels, there is no discrepancy in point of fact. Luke purposely groups his subjects, connecting them in a different way from that of the actual order of events.

The Temptations and Their Counterpart.

Now the Lord's first acts of benevolence and faithfulness, as narrated in the Gospel of John, are the counterpart respectively of His three victories over the Evil One in the wilderness. And in this we can discern a Divine determination that the hidden glories of His triumph over the Adversary should be displayed immediately in His deeds of grace and faithfulness, and in His teaching.

The First Temptation and the First Miracle.

His first victory in the wilderness lay in resisting the Devil's suggestion to turn stones into bread, that is to say, in refusing to transform one substance into another of greater value so as to meet an immediate need. His first public miracle was precisely after this manner, though the substances were different. At the wedding feast in Cana He turned water into wine, and in so doing He performed the very kind of act which He had refused to do at the instigation of Satan. In the Divine counsels the character of His victory over the spiritual foe found its counterpart in His act of blessing at Cana. "This beginning of His signs did Jesus...and manifested His glory" (John 2. 11). That glory, previously unseen by man, which expressed itself in refusal to act in a certain way, was now displayed in a corresponding manner in service to the Father on behalf of men. Surely we may trace a Divine recompense in this, a joy in the display of grace after the trial of conflict.

The Second Temptation and the Temple-Cleansing.

The second way in which the Lord overcame the Adversary in the wilderness was in His refusal to cast Himself down from a pinnacle of the Temple so as to vindicate (probably before the public gaze) the fact of His Divine Sonship. It can scarcely be regarded as an undesigned coincidence that His second recorded public act after the marriage at Cana of Galilee was in connection with the Temple in Jerusalem. Instead of casting Himself down from the outside He cleanses the inside. His faithfulness in the

The Moral Glories of Christ. 53

former case finds its counterpart in His faithfulness in maintaining the character of His Father's House. Instead of relying, at the Devil's suggestion, upon God's provision of angelic care to prevent the destruction of His body, He now predicts the destruction of "the temple of His body," and declares that He will raise it up. Having refused to display His glory by the advice of the Evil One, in the preservation of His body, He will devote it to the redemptive sacrifice of the Cross, and manifest His glory in His resurrection. Satan's scheme to preserve the body of Christ was but a subtle effort to prevent the greater glory of the resurrection of His body. Here again is a Divine compensation. For it was in His resurrection that the Father vindicated His Sonship. "He was declared to be the Son of God . . . by the resurrection of the dead" (Rom. 1. 4).

In the case of the first temptation and the first miracle the Lord, having refused to supply His own needs, displayed, in meeting the needs of others, His sympathy and tenderness; in the second instance, in cleansing the Temple in His zeal for His Father's House, He manifested His holiness and faithfulness.

The Third Temptation, the Kingdom, and Worship.

The third victory in the wilderness was the

Lord's refusal to receive from Satan the kingdoms of this world and their glory, on condition of doing him an act of worship (Matt. 4. 8-10). Here, again, we find a similar correspondence in the narrative in John's Gospel. For the Kingdom of God and the worship of God are the subjects of which the Lord treats respectively in the next events in that Gospel, namely, in His conversations with Nicodemus and the woman of Samaria. The Devil had sought to frustrate the Divinely appointed display of the glories of the Kingdom by an arrangement which would anticipate its manifestation. According to the Divine counsels, the powers of the spiritual kingdom must be in operation first. The Kingdom of God must be in mystery before it comes in manifestation. When the spiritual kingdom, the kingdom which is entered by the new birth, is completed, then will the usurper, over whom the Lord triumphed, be cast out of the earth, and the kingdom of the world which Christ refused at his hands will become His own possession, by the decree and power of God.

How marvellous, again, that to the poor degraded woman of Samaria, the slave of sin and Satan, the Lord should give instruction concerning worship! It cannot have been very long after the time when He repulsed His adversary by His "It is written, thou shalt worship the

Lord thy God," that He spoke to the woman concerning the true worshippers, who "shall worship the Father in Spirit and in truth."

"He that Overcometh."

There are lessons for us in all this, that is to say, in the fact that the moral glories of the Lord in overcoming temptation issued, with such precise correspondence, in the character of His earliest ministry among men. Faithfulness in resisting the spiritual foe is the sure precursor of power in service for God. And the character of the service is often determined by the nature of the victory over temptation. Joseph, who refuses to stain his character and mar his overseership of Potiphar's house by yielding to the enticement of his master's wife, becomes the Prime Minister over the whole country, and receives a wife by royal appointment. Daniel, who refuses to dishonour God by conforming to the arrangements of the Eastern Court and defiling Himself with the king's meat, becomes Governor over the whole province of Babylon and President over the hundred and twenty satraps of the entire dominion. Fidelity to the will of God, under pressure of temptation, brings its recompense in this life, and will receive its eternal reward hereafter. He who in the days of His humiliation resisted every effort to allure Him from the path to the Cross, is "crowned with glory and honour," and from His place of majesty and power encourages His tempted saints to overcome, "even as He overcame." They who refuse to defile their garments here shall walk with Him "in white."

He Who is the Subject of the Gospel records stands therein before the reader as One who belongs to no special type or class of man. Christ is the representative Man. He unites in Himself every trait that is characteristic of man, apart from sin and its effects. Every strong and manly virtue shines in Him, as well as every tender and softer quality. He comprehends in Himself the ideals of both sexes. As Westcott says: "Whatever there is in man, of strength, justice, and wisdom; whatever there is in woman of sensibility, of purity, and insight, is in Christ, without the conditions which hinder among us the development of contrasted virtues in one person. Jesus is the single universal Man, in the closest kinship with men of all time and climates."

The Gospels present Him as One who is free from the characteristic limitations, whether of race, or nation, or family. This is the more remarkable as there was everything, both in nationality and in the family circumstances in which He was born and brought up, conducive to the production of a distinct type. There are two influences which specially make for this.

THE MORAL GLORIES OF CHRIST. 57

They are heredity and environment. Their effects are separative, sectionalizing, isolating.

Heredity.

Christ was born into the Jewish nation. Of all national types the Jewish is one of the most persistent; yet there is nothing in either the character or teachings of Christ which mark Him conspicuously as a Jew. In this He is unique, exceptional. His teachings find an audience which is coextensive with humanity, and an answer in the inner experiences of all men. He is the connecting link between men of the most divergent nationalities. The circumscribing laws of heredity do not find an illustration in Him.

Environment.

Take again the subject of environment. The circumstances and surroundings of a person's upbringing tend to exert a characterizing influence which distinguishes him according to his locality. The district of Galilee was no exception. On the contrary, the references to this place, in the Gospels and the Acts, mark it out particularly as of a specializing character. "Behold, are not all these which speak Galileans?" said the people who were listening to the testimony of the disciples on the day of Pentecost. That the locality was also signalized by provincialisms, is plain from Matthew 26. 73. There was everything, then, in His early environment to affect the life of Christ in such a way as to indicate the place of His upbringing. Yet how free He was from all specialization of this sort!

Consider again the handicraft at which He wrought, the family means of livelihood. After He entered upon His public life and testimony, those who had known Him asked, "Is not this the Carpenter?" (Mark 6. 31). Ordinarily speaking such an environment is not conducive to universality of type. Yet how world-wide are His affinities! The barriers that tend to separate men of one nationality from those of another are broken down in Him. No matter by whom or where the Gospel narratives are read there is nobody who does not find in Him the nearest kinsman, One in whom there is, sin excepted, a point of contact, such as is shared by no other.

THE NINEFOLD FRUIT.

We will now contemplate the moral glories of Christ from another point of view. The Word of God declares that "The fruit of the Spirit is love, joy, peace, longsuffering, kindness, goodness, faithfulness, meekness, temperance (or self-control)," nine virtues combined in a perfect harmony of character. This passage, which speaks indeed of the effects of the Spirit's work in the believer, provides at the same time a commentary upon the character of the Lord as revealed in the Gospels. In His case these moral excellences were the display of glories essential in His Manhood. To illustrate each trait from the records of the four Evangelists would occupy a large volume. We will here consider the witness of Christ Himself to His character in these respects. Nor will space permit us to refer to the whole of His teaching. One passage must suffice. It contains within its compass every trait enumerated in the verse in the Galatians Epistle, and almost, though not precisely, in the same order. It is His discourse to the disciples in the upper room on the night of His betrayal. Here, too, He speaks significantly of fruitfulness. If the disciples are to bear fruit, it will of necessity be the outcome of His own fruitfulness.

The first in the list of virtues spoken of is
Love.
Now in the 15th chapter of John's Gospel the Lord immediately follows His statement as to bearing fruit by speaking of His love. "Herein," He says, "is My Father glorified, that ye bear much fruit, and so shall ye be My disciples. Even as the Father hath loved Me, I also have loved you: abide ye in My love" (chap. 15. 8, 9). His love was not mere sentiment, it consisted in keeping His Father's commandments. And our love is to be no different; it is to express itself in obedience to His own commandments, and so in loving one another (verses 10-12). His was the "greater

love," exhibited in the laying down of His life.
The next item in the fruit of the Spirit is

Joy.

This finds correspondence in the Lord's next utterance, "These things have I spoken unto you, that My joy may be in you" (verse 11). One of His objects in speaking to the disciples was that they might have His joy fulfilled in themselves (chap. 17. 13). His joy lay in abiding in the love of the Father and so in doing His will, and only so can our joy be fulfilled.

The third quality is

Peace.

Of His peace the Lord speaks earlier in His discourse: "Peace I leave with you: My peace I give unto you" (chap. 15. 27). This is "the peace of Christ" of which the apostle writes in Colossians 3. 15 (R.V.), which is to rule, or rather, to arbitrate, in our hearts, removing our anxieties and fears, and settling our troubles. How dark and terrible were the Lord's circumstances on the night of the betrayal! The traitor was already engaged in his murderous plot. The agony of Gethsemane lay immediately before Him, to be followed by the terrible experiences of His trial and the more terrible sufferings of the Cross. All were known to the Lord beforehand. Yet it is in these circumstances that He speaks to the disciples of "My peace."

As we read on in the 15th chapter the other qualities mentioned under the fruit of the Spirit come before us in due order. They are not specifically mentioned, but we cannot read the Lord's words concerning Himself without readily discerning these traits in His character, and especially as He speaks of the treatment He received from men. The world, He says, had hated Him (verse 19), and this in itself serves to remind us of His

Longsuffering.

This is particularly seen in His controversies with the opposing Jews as recorded in John's Gospel, chapters 5 to 11. It was only after they had sinned away all their opportunities that He finally departed from them (chap. 11. 54).

Men had persecuted Him (verse 20). Their persecutions served to draw forth a display of His

Gentleness.

His gentleness, which never ran into weakness, was the expression of His sympathy, His tender compassion for all in feebleness, distress, and need.

In spite of the hardness of heart and the wilful resistance and antagonism of His enemies, He had "come and spoken unto them" (verse 22), and in this He veritably displayed His

Goodness

"Their ill but drew His goodness forth."

In addition to this He had "done among them the works which none other did" (verse 24). In this He exhibited His

Faithfulness.

For all His works were done in "faithfulness and truth" (see Isa. 25. 1, R.V.).

The malice His enemies had displayed against Him had fulfilled as He says, the word that was written in their Law, "They hated Me without a cause" (verse 25), and the trait of character which stands out in Him conspicuously under it all is His

Meekness.

"He was as a Lamb that is led to the slaughter, and as a sheep that before her shearers is dumb," "The meekness and gentleness" of Christ fastened themselves indelibly upon Paul's heart. How tellingly he makes them the basis of his appeal to the Corinthian saints to rectify their relations with himself! (2 Cor. 10. 1). Christ's meekness was never disunited from His Majesty. The incomparable splendour of His greatness shone especially through His meekness. He gained the mastery over injustice while suffering it. Never were words more impressively grand and yet tender in their meekness and love than when, while undergoing crucifixion, He said, "Father forgive them: for they know not what they do."

The last of the nine in the Galatians Epistle is

The Moral Glories of Christ. 63

Self-control.

Strikingly is this exhibited in the Lord's character in the discourse in the upper room! How patient were His dealings with these disciples, with their misunderstandings and slowness of heart! How much He had to tell them! His heart was yearning to unlock its secrets to them in fuller measure. "I have yet many things to say unto you," He says, "but ye cannot bear them now" (chap. 16. 12). He felt indeed a tender sympathy toward them in their weakness, and hence His self-restraint. But this is only one instance of that same quality which manifests itself throughout the discourse, with a sublime majesty, an inexpressible grandeur.

All that perfection of character which is summed up in the phrase "the fruit of the Spirit" stands forth in its full beauty of combined virtues in the self-witness of the Lord's teaching here, as indeed it does in all His ways. The effect upon the disciples, itself an evidence of the ascendancy the Lord gained over them, was at the same time a proof of His moral strength. He who at first was recognized by them as a Teacher, not differing much perhaps from a Rabbi, was now their Lord. Is His ascendancy absolute over our own hearts? Is His character being stamped upon us, changing us from glory to glory, as into His own image? May it be so for His Name's sake!

CHAPTER VII.

The Atoning Sacrifice of Christ.

THE object for which the Son of God came into the world is conveyed in His Name "Jesus," which signifies "Jehovah (is) salvation." The inspired interpretation of it is, "For it is He that (or, literally, He Himself) shall save His people from their sins." In the words of one of His Apostles, "Christ Jesus came into the world to save sinners" (1 Tim. 1. 15). The means of accomplishing this end was His Death. He said that He had come "to give His life a ransom for many" (Matt. 20. 28), that He would "lay down His life for the sheep" (John 10. 11-15). He was manifested "to put away sin by the sacrifice of Himself" (Heb. 9. 26). His sacrifice was **Divinely Preordained.**
Christ was "delivered up by the determinate counsel and foreknowledge of God" (Acts 2. 23). His death was therefore not accidental, it was an essential part of the Divine scheme of Redemption. He Himself said to His disciples, "Thus it is written that Christ should suffer, and rise again from the dead the third day:

The Atoning Sacrifice of Christ. 65

and that repentance and remission of sins should be preached in His Name" (Luke 24. 46, 47).

He came, then, not merely to teach men how to live, though that He did, nor so to tell them about God's love that they might forsake sin. He came that "through death" He might bring salvation to men (Heb. 2. 14, 15). He "suffered for sins once, the Righteous for the unrighteous, that He might bring us to God" (1 Peter 3. 18). His sacrifice was therefore

Vicarious,

and this is borne out by the following facts:—Christ lived a sinless life, even His adversaries and His critics being witnesses. On this ground alone freedom from death was His perfect right, and that by Divine decree. The Law of God promised life to him who fulfilled it. Alone of men Christ absolutely carried out the conditions. Yet He died! Now His death was not simply the result of His encountering human antagonism. He could have avoided it. This He demonstrated when His conspirators came to bind Him (John 18. 6; cp. 8. 59; 10. 39; Luke 4. 29, 30), and thus He confirmed His own statement, "I lay down My life, that I may take it again. No one taketh it away from Me, but I lay it down of Myself. I have power to lay it down, and I have power to take it again. This commandment received I from My Father" (John 10. 17, 18). To the judge who sentenced Him, He said, "Thou couldest have no power against Me, except it were given thee from above" (chap. 19. 11). His death was unique, in that, in His case alone, the choice lay between dying and never dying at all. He could have refrained from drinking the bitter cup. It follows that, death being the consequence of sin (Rom. 5. 12; 6. 23), the death of Christ was substitutionary. "He died to atone for sins not His own." "He was wounded for our transgressions," "Jehovah laid on Him the iniquity of us all" (Isa. 53. 5, 6).

The Character of Sin.

False ideas of the Atonement are largely due to light views both of sin and of the holiness of God. Sin is neither a temporary misadventure, nor is it simply a disease or a disaster, nor again is it "a necessary stage to higher things." "Sin is lawlessness" (1 John 3. 4, R.V.). It is disregard of the will of God. It is due to unbelief (Rom. 14. 23; John 16. 9). God, as moral Governor of the universe, gave to man a Law which was the reflection of His righteous character, a Law the fulfilment of which was for man's highest welfare. The breach of that Law was culpable disregard of the Creator's beneficent will, and rendered man liable to God's righteous retribution. The very attributes of God demanded the execution of the penalty. To refrain from exacting it would be to nullify the Law and belie the Divine character. Divine forgiveness could be imparted only in a manner consistent with God's claims of justice, the rectitude of His administration and His irreconcilability to evil.

The Person Requisite.

Atonement is impossible to man. Repentance would be ineffectual, for it could not restore the broken legal relation to God. An amended life could not do so, for it could not cancel previous guilt. Man in his unregenerate state cannot please God (Rom. 8. 8). Nor could the sinner make atonement by death, either for himself or for his fellow men. Expiation is demanded on a righteous basis. In order to make such expiation a Person was required who had an adequate apprehension of the nature and claims of God. He must likewise be proved to be free from all taint of sin. He must be one who would bear the curse of the broken Law, or his suffering would be on his own account, and consequently no judicial advantage could accrue to others therein. He must, moreover, put himself in connection with the Law, that he might be tested thereby.

Now there was only one Being who could and did fulfil all these conditions, and that was the Son of God. Being Himself one in Godhood with the Father, He, and He alone, had a perfect understanding of the nature and claims of God.

The other conditions were likewise fulfilled by Him, for, though He was Himself the Creator and Sustainer of the Universe (Col. 1. 16, 17), Whose goings forth had been "from of old, from everlasting" (Micah 5. 2), He became Incarnate, was born under the Law, submitted to all its tests and fulfilled it without deviation, "becoming obedient, even unto death, yea, the death of the Cross." Such a One alone could bear our sin. And this He did, "being made sin for us,.... that we might become the righteousness of God in Him" (2 Cor. 5. 21). It was necessary that God should deal with Him, His sinless Son, as He would with sin. That is the significance of the lifting up of the brazen serpent, as the Lord Himself explained to Nicodemus. Jehovah made "His soul an offering for sin" (Isa. 53. 10).

In this way alone could God "Himself be just and the Justifier" of the sinner. This is the grand plan of Divine grace in the Atonement. Whereas "all have sinned, and fall short of the glory of God," man can through faith be "justified freely by His grace through the redemption that is in Christ Jesus." For God "set Him forth to be a propitiation, through faith, by His blood ...that He might Himself be just and the Justifier of Him that hath faith in Jesus" (Rom. 3. 23-26). "He (this word has the emphasis) is the propitiation for our sins" (1 John 2. 2).

An Objection.

Objection is raised against the character of the Atonement, in that such a substitutionary death for sin is, it is urged, impossible, since guilt is untransferable, and the innocent remains innocent. The objection is invalid. Personal blameworthiness is indeed untransferable, but to suffer for the sins of another is possible to anyone and is a common fact in human experience. It was to deliver men from a deserved penalty that Christ suffered. For this He bore the stroke of Divine justice. "Jehovah laid on Him the iniquity of us all." There are depths in the sufferings of Christ on the Cross which the human mind can never fathom None will ever be able to measure or explain the mystery of that anguish which, under the weight of sin and the wrath due to it, drew forth the cry, "My God, My God, why hast Thou forsaken Me." Nor will anyone ever fully apprehend the other great truth, equally essential in the doctrine of the Atonement, that "God was in Christ, reconciling the world unto Himself." This alone precludes any attempt to reduce the subject to terms of mere human jurisprudence, or to explain the work of the Cross by any illustration of the law courts.

The facts of the unity of the Son with the Father show at what an incalculable cost God gave up His Son to die for us. "He spared not His own

Son." "Herein was the love of God manifested in us (*i.e.*, in regard to us), that God hath sent His only begotten Son." "Herein is love...that He loved us and sent His Son to be the propitiation for our sins" (1 John 4. 8-10).

Another Objection.

Again, it is urged that a substitutionary sacrifice is contrary to moral rectitude, since for another person to die to secure freedom from future punishment could effect no radical change in the moral character of the guilty. That, however, is contrary to Scripture and to the facts of Christian experience. The Gospel cries out against continuance in sin. The death of Christ enables the believer to say with the Apostle Paul, "I have been crucified with Christ...who loved Me and gave Himself up for me" (Gal. 2. 20), to reckon himself to be "dead to sin" and "alive unto God," and so to walk "in newness of life." In suffering judgment and death to deliver us from the merited penalty, Christ suffered also to deliver us from sin, which was the cause of our condemnation. Such love begets a love that hates the sin on account of which the Saviour died. Again, Christ did not die merely to show God's benevolence towards man. His life alone could have done that, and then the full expression of God's character would not have been exhibited. Nor was His death merely a manifestation of God's love. His death revealed God's justice in carrying out therein all that was due to sin, and His love and mercy in doing so in the Person of His Son. "God commendeth His own love toward us, in that, while we were yet sinners, Christ died for us" (Rom. 5. 8). Thus the Divine love glorified the Divine holiness and righteousness. "Mercy and truth met together. Righteousness and peace kissed each other."

That Christ became a sin-offering for us, that we might be delivered from the merited execution of the sentence due to our guilt, involved no compromise of the righteousness of Divine administration. In inflicting the sentence on the sinner's voluntary Surety, Jehovah, "while He cleared the sinner, did not clear his sins," but executed His righteous sentence upon them. The ends of Divine justice were fully assured.

The Nature of His Death.

His Death then was not that of a martyr to a cause. Nor did He die merely to secure a blessing for man. His Death was expiatory. He became Incarnate, partaking of flesh and blood, in order to present Himself to be made sin and to become a curse for us, and so to remove the curse which was ours by the righteous judgment of God. Voluntarily He submitted to the death of the Cross in order that on a righteous basis man might be restored to fellowship with God.

Again, His Death fulfilled, and more than fulfilled, all that was foreshadowed by the offerings of animal sacrifices upon the altar. The death must be by the shedding of blood. "The life of the flesh is in the blood." Man had forfeited his life through sin. Death came by sin. Hence the Divine appointment of animal sacrifices, which, though they were substitutionary, could not themselves clear the conscience from sin. The blood of bulls and goats could not take away sins (Heb. 10. 4). No animal sacrifices could provide atonement for a sinner's future sins. The blood of Christ "cleanseth from all sin;" it has made a complete atonement.

Reconciliation.

The words in the original, rendered "atonement" and "reconciliation," are not to be explained by the English "at-one-ment." The Hebrew word denotes "to cover," *i.e.*, by interposition for the removal of guilt. The Greek word suggests propitiation, the gaining of pardon. Christ did not die to reconcile God. "God was in Christ, reconciling the world." Not that God was reconciled to man's sin. That could never be. And as to His attitude towards the sinner, while His love provided a remedy in that "while we were yet sinners Christ died for the ungodly," yet the wrath of God still abides on him who does not believe on the Son (John 3. 36, *margin*). The sinner is therefore called to be reconciled to God, not "to bend his pride to God's benevolence," but to secure His pardon.

Redemption.

On this ground it is that God pardons the guilty, a pardon complete and immediate upon acceptance of Christ. Thus God delivers from the death sentence and gives the believing sinner acceptance in Christ. This is redemption. In Christ "we have our redemption through His blood (*i.e.*, His death by the shedding of His blood), the forgiveness of our trespasses, according to the riches of His grace" (Eph. 1. 7).

Redemption has two sides to it, one the ransom paid, the other the liberation of the sinner from his position of condemnation and death. The two are to one another as cause and effect. The ransom price of the blood of Christ was paid to the claims of Divine holiness and justice. The ransom was paid for all men. But all men will not accept the provision made. Only those who do so are actually redeemed and find in Christ their Substitute.

The Scope of the Atonement.

The language of Scripture is precise here. Only twice is the word *anti*, "instead of," which denotes actual substitution, found in the New Testament, namely, in Matthew 20. 28, and Mark 10. 45, and there it is "a ransom for (instead of) *many.*" In 1 Timothy 2. 6 the word *antilutron* occurs: "Who gave Himself a ransom (*antilutron,* a substitutionary ransom) for (*huper,* on behalf of) all." That expresses the substitutionary character of the ransom, but the Apostle does not say "instead of all." The provision made was *on behalf of* "all," it is *instead of* "many," that is to say, those who are no longer in death and condemnation, because, through acceptance of Christ as their Substitute, they are actually delivered from that position.

"He is the propitiation (*i.e.*, the Person through whom by His expiatory death God shows mercy to sinners)...for the sins of the whole world." The actual remission takes place only in the case of those who avail themselves of the propitiation. Only believers can say that their sins have been atoned for by Christ. Those who refuse it must perish eternally. There is no Scripture to show that Christ bore away every man's sins on the Cross. John the Baptist's statement, "Behold the Lamb of God which taketh away the sin of the world," means that sin was so dealt with there, that now all who accept God's terms may be freed from guilt, and that hereafter in the new heavens and new earth there will be no trace of sin. Christ was manifested "to put away sin" by the sacrifice of Himself" (Heb. 9. 26). We must in such verses distinguish

The Atoning Sacrifice of Christ.

between sin and sins (1 Cor. 15. 3). Christ "died for our sins," "suffered for sins" (1 Peter 3. 18). The provision is universal, the application is made good only in the case of those who receive Christ by faith, on the ground of His finished work on the Cross.

CHAPTER VIII.

The Resurrection of Christ.

THE Resurrection of Christ is the keystone of the arch of historical evidences relating to His Person and work. The fact of His Resurrection confirms the truth of His Deity, His supernatural Birth, His sinlessness, and His substitutionary Sacrifice on the Cross. Apart from His Resurrection there would be no Christian faith to declare. There would remain a system of morals, but that is not Christianity. Christianity involves the operation of a Personal power producing effects inexplicable by the laws of nature. The very basis of Christianity is supernatural. Admit the existence of God, and thereby is admitted that miracles are likely exhibitions of His power. Disprove the possibility or credibility of the supernatural, and the foundations of the Christian faith vanish. The message of the Resurrection comprehends and sums up all that the Gospel declares. If the Resurrection is not a fact there is no Gospel to preach. "If Christ hath not been raised, then is our preaching vain, your faith also is vain (*kenos*, void of result)," says the apostle (1 Cor. 15. 14). Again, "if Christ hath not been raised, your faith is vain (*mataios*, void of reality); ye are yet in your sins" (v. 17).

Christ's Resurrection was at once **The Vindication of His Divine Sonship.** He was "declared to be the Son of God with power, according to the Spirit of holiness, by the resurrection of the dead" (Rom. 1. 4). It was also the vindication of His sinlessness, of which, indeed, it was the inevitable complement. Life was assured to him who fulfilled the Law. Christ's perfect fulfilment of it not only involved the vicarious character of His Death, for there was nothing in Him for which to atone, it also rendered resurrection His presumptive right. In this He stands alone. Being God's "Holy One" it was not possible for Him "to be holden of death" (Acts 2. 24). The Psalmist had prophesied of Him, "Thou wilt not leave My soul in Sheol: neither wilt Thou suffer Thine Holy One to see corruption. Thou wilt shew Me the path of life" (Psa. 16. 10, 11).

Again, His Resurrection was **The Ratification of the Atoning Efficacy of His Death.** "He was delivered up for (on account of) our trespasses, and was raised for (on account of) our justification." Our justification having been secured in His death—for "we are justified by His blood" (Rom. 5. 9)—God raised Him from the dead. The significance attaching to the Death of Christ finds its adequate explanation in His Resurrection. His Resurrection was also the display of His authority over death. All others had been, or will be, raised solely by a power from without. Not so with the Lord. He was raised by His own power as well as by that of the Father. Of His body He said to His foes, "Destroy this temple, and in three days I will raise it up" (John 2. 19). This itself constitutes an inarguable testimony to His Resurrection as being that of His body and not merely that of His spirit. Of His life He said, "I have power to lay it down, and I have power to take it again. This commandment received I from My Father" (chap. 10. 18). As the ascended and exalted One He declares to the beloved Apostle, "I am the first and the last, and the Living One: and I was dead, and behold, I am alive for evermore, and I have the keys of death and Hades" (Rev. 1. 17, 18). **The Basis of the Gospel.**

The first preachers of the Gospel made the fact of Christ's Resurrection the foundation of all their testimony. Peter bases upon it the fact of the sending of the Spirit at Pentecost (Acts 2. 33), the power of faith (chap. 3. 15, 16), repentance, forgiveness of sins, and salvation (chap. 3. 30-38 with 4. 12). So with Paul; the Gospel he preached was that "Christ died for our sins, according to

THE RESURRECTION OF CHRIST. 79

the Scriptures; and that He was buried; and that He hath been raised on the third day, according to the Scriptures" (1 Cor. 15. 3, 4). The confession of Jesus as Lord, and the belief that God raised Him from the dead are, he says, essential to salvation (Rom. 10. 9). His Resurrection is the guarantee of that of the saints (Rom. 8. 11; 1 Cor. 15. 20-23), and of their complete reunion (1 Thess. 4. 14), and of the overthrow of God's foes and the establishment of His Kingdom (1 Cor. 15. 25). It provides the Divine assurance that by Him God will judge the world in righteousness (Acts 17. 31). The Resurrection of Christ then was both the climax of past developments of grace and the beginning of new developments of life, involving the formation, progress, and destiny of the Church, and the eventual deliverance of Creation from the bondage of corruption.

The Evidence.

The limited character of the present article precludes anything like a review of the evidences of the Lord's Resurrection, nor can we here dwell upon the subject of the well established veracity and integrity of the New Testament records. Any difficulties which are considered to beset the character of the evidence are far less than those relative to other historical facts. In no other case are there so many convergent lines of evidence. With what convincing naturalness, for instance, the fact emerges in each Gospel narrative from those events which led up to it! The way in which the writers treat it is as unaffected and inartificial as everything else they record. They evince no such idea as that this event, though unique and startling in itself, requires any more detailed authentication than the undoubted facts that Christ lived and died. There is no attempt at impressiveness.

Take, for instance, the discovery of
The Cloths in the Empty Tomb.
The body of the Lord had been bound* in linen cloths with about one hundred pounds weight of spices (John 19. 39, 40). John describes Peter as entering into the tomb, and seeing the linen cloths lying, and the napkin that had been around the Lord's head, not lying with the linen cloths, but 'rolled round in a place by itself.' There is no suggestion that the head napkin had been folded up and put in another part of the tomb. That cloth was still lying in its folded shape where the head had been. So were the body cloths. Neither friends nor foes had touched them. Friends would not have moved the garments from the body; foes would not have left them in the

---

* John here uses the word *deō* (to bind), the same word as in the case of Lazarus (11. 44), and as in the act of those who with hands of hate bound Christ as a captive (18. 12-24). Matthew uses *entulissō*, "to fold round," as does John later in 20. 7; Mark uses *eneileō*, "to wind round closely." Evidently John's first word *deō*, in 19. 39, is used purposively, in order to set in greater contrast in 20. 7 the evidences of the Resurrection as seen by him in the position of the cloths.

THE RESURRECTION OF CHRIST. 81

position in which they were found. Nor again was there any indication of a struggle to obtain release. The Lord had simply left the cloths as they had been bound around Him. This is the significance of John's statements as to the binding of the body and the position of the cloths, and of his testimony concerning himself, "he saw* and believed." The evidence was clear. What had occurred was not a removal of the body, but a resurrection. How marvellous was the sight! How unique the event! Yet how simply the narrative is told! And this is characteristic of the records not only of the Resurrection, but of the Lord's subsequent appearances to His disciples. The writers obviously are not seeking to add to literature, but are simply recording facts which they know to be true. Their sincerity cannot be doubted. The character of the evidences makes it impossible that they were victims of delusions. There was nothing in their thoughts and experiences which would inspire an ardent desire for such an event and so an anticipation of it. Whenever the Lord had spoken about it they did not understand Him (Luke 18. 34). His closest disciples did not anticipate it, yet only a few days afterwards the whole company were absolutely assured of its certainty.

---
* In reference to Peter, John uses two other words for seeing, *blepō* (verse 5), which means the act of seeing (cp. ver. 1), and *theoreō* (v. 6), to view attentively (cp. vv. 12-14): in reference to himself he uses *eidō*, which indicates a perception of the meaning of what is seen.

The Effect on the Disciples.

Moreover, the occasions of His appearances were many and varied, and were of sufficient length for considerable intercourse and personal contact. The overwhelming power of these realities produced such a conviction, that their character became changed, their faith was transformed, and a few days after the final evidence had been provided they were all making it the business of their lives to proclaim the facts. Again, they were men of intelligence and probity. Their very incredulity marks them as the victims neither of superstition nor imposition. Besides, they had no worldly advantage to gain from the publication of the Resurrection. The very reverse. They knew that they must suffer for their testimony.

Take again the testimony of Paul. The truth which he himself had "received" he taught with the intenseness of a personal conviction gained through experience. "He appeared to me also," he says. And again, "Have not I seen Jesus our Lord?" He does not labour to prove the truth of the Lord's Resurrection. His argument in 1 Corinthians 15 is against a denial of the resurrection of the dead, though not of Christ's Resurrection. There is no evidence that the latter was denied, and so he uses the common belief of that fact as a proof of a future resurrection of the saints.

The Veracity of the Writers.

The narratives in the Four Gospels are clearly independent one of another, and yet are harmonious. Whatever differences there are, there are no discrepancies. Careful study of the details makes clear both the consistency and the independence of the records. If the story were invented it must have been either in collusion or independently. That the records were not fabricated by collusion is clear from the apparent discrepancies. That they were independent fabrications is impossible. The points of agreement are too many.

Again, the character of the records bears irrefutable testimony to the evidence as having been derived from eye-witnesses. There are a number of incidental details which serve to establish the veracity of the writers. For instance, that Christ was not recognised first when He appeared to the disciples (Luke 24. 16; John 21. 4), and again that He is not stated to have appeared to one of His enemies, or represented as confounding them by such a manifestation, are all contrary to the fabrication theory. An appearance to His foes, with its convincing effects, would have been a great point with one who was inventing the story. That Christ is recorded as having appeared solely to His followers substantiates the genuineness of the narratives. So also does the very limited number of the occasions of His appearing during the forty days. Men who were fabricating the story would have elaborated such manifestations both in number and point of detail. They would have depicted Christ as appearing in a body as glorious as on the occasion of the Transfiguration. There is nothing of this, however. With perfect naturalness the Lord shows His wound prints. The Roman spear, the *pilum*, had a shaft four inches wide, and inflicted a wound so large that a hand might be thrust into it. Even had He not died already, survival was impossible; yet He appears in perfect strength, not as a man miraculously saved from dying of wounds, but as One who had overcome death in resurrection.

The brevity of the narrative in each case is a testimony to its being a presentation of facts. Then, too, the modes of action on the part of the disciples in connection with their discovery of the empty tomb, and the subsequent details, are all in keeping with the differing characteristics of the persons as exhibited in the Gospels. The incidental touches of colouring in the picture are perfectly true to life.

Not merely a Spiritual Resurrection.

The theory that the Resurrection of Christ was merely spiritual represents an old error which has reappeared with widespread propagation in recent

THE RESURRECTION OF CHRIST.

times. The teaching of Scripture entirely refutes the error. Firstly, when the Apostle asks, "How are the dead raised," he says at the same time, "With what manner of body do they come?" Then, using the illustration of the death of seed sown in the ground, he says, "But God giveth it a body even as it hath pleased Him, and to each seed a body of its own...So also is the resurrection of the dead" (1 Cor. 15. 35-42). So then the dead saints are to be raised with bodies. Now their resurrection is to be in the likeness of Christ's (Rom. 6. 5). It follows that His was a bodily resurrection. *

Secondly, the Apostle speaks of Christ as "the last Adam," "the second Man." Now man as such is constituted a tripartite being, body, soul, and spirit. This then is the constitution of the Second Man, the Adamic Head of the new race of the redeemed. His being, as possessed of true manhood, is conditioned both by His Incarnation and His Death, and His Resurrection. Thirdly, when speaking of His Deity the Apostle says, "In Him dwelleth all the fulness of the Godhead bodily" (Col. 2. 9). As Moule says, "He rose, identical yet with differences. His body risen was the same as His body buried. But we need not insist on an identity of particles, which certainly is not necessary to our own continuous

---

*See also what is said above concerning John 2. 19.

bodily identity. That identity appears to rest on personal spiritual identity. The sameness of a hand at two times of life lies, not in its consisting of the same matter, but in its holding the same relation to the same spirit. What the Gospels make clear, on the one hand, is the reality and permanence of Jesus Christ's resurrection body, under tests of sense, to which the all-truthful Lord Himself appeals. On the other hand it is plain that the body's mode of being and action was new. It appears that it was capable of transition, inconceivable to us, through material mass."

Fourthly, the Gospel records bear clear witness against the theory of a mere spiritual resurrection. "See My hands and My feet, that it is I Myself:" He says to His disciples, "handle Me and see; for a spirit hath not flesh and bones, as ye behold Me having" (Luke 24. 39). His appearances to His disciples are not to be explained by the supposition of temporary materializations. Such an idea is a gratuitous and unfounded assumption, representing the unsuccessful attempts of finite minds to explain the infinite and almighty. All that belonged to the Lord's humanity was retained in resurrection, while at the same time all was transfigured. The fact that He vanished at will does not involve the impossibility of His being permanently corporeal. His raised and transfigured body was and is under conditions not expressed by the laws which govern this creation. The Lord entered on His new mode of existence with His perfect Manhood in permanent completeness. **The Effects.**

In the risen, exalted Christ our whole life and being are centred. Our bodies are "members of Christ" (1 Cor. 6. 15), and the Church is the body of Christ (Eph. 1. 23), in whom the members find a common principle of action in the discharge of their varying functions, a union in life which lies deeper than the controversies which here tend to divide them, a fulness of truth and power which consecrates their beings to their living Redeemer. "The body is...for the Lord; and the Lord for the body; and God both raised up the Lord, and will raise up us through His power" (1 Cor. 6. 13, 14).

Such are the effects of a teaching, itself the outcome of the solid conviction of the truth of Christ's Resurrection. His Resurrection was the beginning of a new and permanent relation between the Lord and His people, a relation yet to be manifested in their resurrection life and glory and in the establishment of His Kingdom on earth. He is the "faithful Witness, the Firstborn of the dead, and the Ruler of the kings of the earth." "To Him be the glory and the dominion for ever and ever. Amen."

CHAPTER IX.

The Ascension of Christ.

THE occasion of the Lord's Ascension was the tenth recorded appearance to His disciples after His Resurrection, though the New Testament Scriptures do not indicate that there were no other appearances. In the enumeration given in 1 Corinthians 15 the instance mentioned in verse 7, when Christ appeared "to all the Apostles" was no doubt that which issued in the Ascension, as recorded in considerable detail in the last chapter of Luke's Gospel and in the first of the Acts. It receives but a brief mention at the close of the Gospel of Mark, in a statement quite consistent with those of Luke. The brevity of the record in Mark's Gospel is no indication of ignorance of the facts on his part.

The First and the Fourth Gospels.

Again, that Matthew and John do not narrate the Ascension, affords no justification for the inference which has been drawn therefrom against its historioity. With both writers the Ascension was clearly a matter of course, following naturally upon the Resurrection. The close of Matthew's Gospel makes plain that in the writer's mind the Ascension was imminent. Moreover he records

Christ's declaration to Caiaphas, "Henceforth ye shall see the Son of Man sitting at the right hand of power, and coming on the clouds of Heaven" (chap. 26. 64). John tells us of the Lord's statement to the disciples that they would see Him "ascending where He was before" (chap. 6. 62), and His words to Mary Magdalene, "Touch Me not (or rather, 'do not cling to Me'); for I am not yet ascended unto the Father: but go unto My brethren, and say to them, I ascend unto My Father and your Father and My God and your God" (chap. 20. 17).

The Gospel of Luke.

Luke's record passes at once from the day of the Resurrection to that of the Ascension, whereas in the Acts he states explicitly that Christ appeared to the disciples during forty days, at the end of which he gives full details of the Ascension. There is, however, no discrepancy between the narratives. There is no hint whatever that Luke intended in his later account to correct anything in the former. The evidence is to the contrary. For he says that his former treatise embraced "all that Jesus began both to do and to teach, until the day in which He was received up." Plainly, therefore, though in the Gospel he did not specify the time, he intended the Ascension to be regarded as having taken place after the interval mentioned. He certainly was not speaking of the Ascension as occurring on the evening of the day when Christ arose, and as there must have been an interval, there is no difficulty in supposing one of forty days in the Gospel narrative.

The Character of the Records.

The same simplicity, sincerity, and dignity which are conspicuous features of the records of the Lord's Resurrection, characterize those of His Ascension. To a reader who looks for grandeur and imagery the narrative would be disappointing. How naturally the story is told! How briefly too! The circumstances could have filled volumes had the writers been mere historians. Here again is that marvellous economy of detail, combined with sufficiency for faith, which marks the historical parts of Scripture as essentially doctrinal, and makes the Bible unique. The more the spiritually interested mind dwells upon the narratives, the more manifest are the inherent glory of the event and the spiritual instruction provided in the records. Certainly a master hand is narrating the incident. Like the Resurrection itself and the Lord's subsequent appearances, the great event was hidden from the world. Conviction of sin and of the truths of redemption were not to be borne in upon the hearts of men by means of an outward display of the Lord's Person and glory. The

THE ASCENSION OF CHRIST.

Divine wisdom had planned a more effectual means than that. Unregenerate humanity needs something more than the manifestation of Divine glory to accomplish the work of grace in the heart.

The Place.

We may gather from Luke's narratives that the disciples had assembled in Jerusalem by the Lord's appointment (Acts 1. 12 says they returned there), and that after appearing in their midst He led them forth to the Mount of Olives, until they were "over against Bethany" (Luke 1. 50), a place dear to His heart by the ties of hospitality and friendship. There, where a home had been opened to Him in the days of His public life and testimony, He would now ascend to His own Home, the Father's dwelling place on high. From that mountain, too, the garden slope of which had often witnessed His prayers, and finally His deep prostration and agony, He would now arise to His highest exaltation, to minister thence to His followers in their sufferings and sorrows.

The Disciples.

Though there is no hint that the disciples were immediately anticipating the event, yet He had fully prepared them for what was to come, banishing their misconceptions and establishing their faith. He had opened their minds to understand the Scriptures concerning Him, had foretold the character of the work that lay before them, preventing any immature enthusiasm which might impel them to separate and undertake their appointed enterprise without the power of the promised Spirit, assuring them that the testimony of John the Baptist was about to be fulfilled and that they would be "baptized with the Holy Ghost not many days hence." With His own exquisite skill and tenderness He had disengaged their thoughts from the freshly awakened anticipation that the kingdom was immediately to be restored to Israel, and had imbued them with a due consciousness of the nature and purpose of the work appointed to them and the power requisite for it (Acts 1. 4-8). He had given them the promise of a Kingdom far surpassing their own expectations and had now prepared them for that path of faith and love, patient suffering and invincible hope, which would lead to that Kingdom.

The Event.

And now with the significant words upon His lips, "in Jerusalem and all Judæa and Samaria, and unto the uttermost parts of the earth," indicating the outgoing of His thoughts to the lost world for which He had given His life, the transcendent moment came. His conversation suddenly passed into words of benediction. Lifting up His hands upon them in an act of blessing, He parted from them, ascending in

The Ascension of Christ.

sublime and noiseless majesty until "a cloud received Him out of their sight." Thence immediately He "passed through the heavens" (Heb. 4. 14) and "sat down at the right hand of the Throne of God" (chap. 12. 2).

The Evidences.

His departure from the world was in keeping with the circumstances of His life on earth. No pomp and ceremony attended His exit. No multitude assembled to witness the startling spectacle. The evidences of the fact of His Ascension were to depend, not on that which would appeal to the natural mind, but on the Spirit-empowered witness of His followers. The evidences are as reliable as those for the Resurrection. The account both in the Gospel of Luke and in the Acts, is that of one who, if he did not see the event, at least heard it from one who had done so. Every detail bears the stamp of genuineness, and imparts the character of undeniable credibility to the whole narrative. The subsequent descent of the Holy Spirit, the apostolic witness, the testimony of Stephen at his martyrdom, of Paul at his conversion, and of John in the Apocalypse, as to their having individually seen the ascended Lord, all add their confirmation to the angelic testimony immediately given in response to the worship and the upward gaze of the disciples after the cloud had received the Lord out of their sight. For them no lingering doubt, no lurking suspicion remained. It was "with great joy" that they returned to Jerusalem.

The Effects.

Little as they had apprehended His statements in the upper room that it would be expedient for Him to go away, they were now to realise the full significance of the fact. The endowment of the Personal power of the Holy Spirit, the diffusion of the spiritual Presence of Christ Himself in the hearts of believers, the experience of all that the authority of His Headship in the glory meant, as well as His gracious ministry as the Shepherd and Bishop of their souls, and in addition the assurance that this same Jesus, who had gone into Heaven, would come again in like manner as they had seen Him go, all this, and much more besides, not only removed the pain of separation, but filled them with abiding peace, imperishable joy, and unconquerable endurance.

The Person.

As His Resurrection was corporeal* so was His Ascension. His was a spiritual body—a body, not a spirit—free from all limitations imposed by natural conditions, yet still bearing the marks of His crucifixion and of the spear-wound in His side. No dematerialized Being entered Heaven. The Lord was still truly Man and as such was

---

* See the chapter on the "Resurrection," page 76.

The Ascension of Christ. 95

possessed of all the constitution and attributes of man—body, soul, and spirit. When the Apostle says, "He that descended is the same also that ascended" (Eph. 4. 10), he is simply stating the fact of the Lord's unchanged Personality. He also states that the One who was "received up in glory" was "He who was manifested in the flesh" (1 Tim. 3. 16). Not only was His Personality unchanged, but the corporeal nature which He had assumed in Incarnation, so far from being discarded, remained in that same transformed condition into which His body was changed in Resurrection by the Almighty power of God, who "raised Him from the dead and made Him to sit at His right hand in the heavenly places" (Eph. 1. 20, 21).

The Dispensational Significance.

His Ascension was both the crowning evidence of the completeness and value of His redeeming work on the Cross, and at the same time marked an epoch in human history relative to the work of the Gospel and the formation of the Church. For now, the Father having put "all things in subjection under His feet," "gave Him to be Head over all things to the Church" (Eph. 1. 22). "When He ascended on high He led captivity captive,* and gave gifts unto men." The Ascen-

---

*It has been supposed that this suggests that the saints of former ages who were in Sheol were now set free therefrom and brought by the Lord into the very presence of the Throne of God. Possibly this is so.

sion, then, marked a turning point in the Divine dispensations. Hitherto God had had a visible dwelling place on earth. Now all was to be changed. He was about to adopt another mode of tabernacling among men, that of the indwelling of the Spirit in His saints, whether individual or collective. Now had come the time when "the Lord dwelleth not in temples made with hands" (Acts 17. 24). The external, the ceremonial, the ritualistic in worship must now yield place to the spiritual. "The hour had come when the true worshippers must worship the Father in spirit and in truth." Finally, the Ascension of the Lord both marks the fact that the saints are already spiritually raised and seated with Him in the heavenly places, and is the guarantee of their ascension in one united, redeemed, and glorified company when His resurrection shout is heard, and He receives them to be for ever with Himself.

CHAPTER X.

The High Priesthood of Christ.

THE glories of the High Priesthood of Christ were prefigured in a twofold way in the distinct priesthoods of Melchizedek and Aaron. Both were required in order to set forth the perfections of the dignity and ministry of Christ. We can here enter only briefly into these aspects of the subject. To begin with, let us notice how the Epistle to the Hebrews points to the first, and perhaps the greatest, teaching of the Old Testament regarding it, so as to set forth the glories of the Melchizedek order of Christ's priesthood as superior to those of the Aaronic order. This presentation in Hebrews provides at the same time many a clue as to the typical character of the Aaronic priesthood, as set forth in connection with the Tabernacle, the consideration of which would overstep the limits of this chapter.

The superiority of

The Melchizedek Order

of Christ's Priesthood is vividly brought out in the seventh chapter. The ancient King-priest is there seen in the mysterious majesty of his person and in the dignified grace of his ministry. We are shown how his biography, given in Genesis 14, was so framed, both by omission and by insertion of detail, that he might prefigure the Person and work of Christ. His regal name, "King of righteousness," and his locality, Salem (or peace), show how the Priesthood of the Lord Jesus is characterised by peace bestowed on a basis of Divine righteousness. The parentage of Melchizedek, the length of his ministry, and his death are all withheld. And thus, by curtailment of the narrative, he is "made like" Him who, in point of fact, as "the Son of God," is without beginning of days or end of life.

The superiority of Christ's Priesthood is next seen with reference to Melchizedek's ministry.

Firstly, under the Law the people paid tithes to the Levitical priests. But Abraham, their forefather, paid tithes to Melchizedek. So virtually, Levi paid tithes to him (vv. 4-9).

Secondly, Abraham was blessed by Melchizedek, and the lesser is blessed by the greater (v. 7).

Thirdly, those who received tithes under the Law were "men that die;" not so with the record concerning Melchizedek (v. 8).

Fourthly, Christ sprang from the royal tribe of Judah, which had no connection with the Levitical priesthood; and a change in the order of the priesthood necessitates a change in regard to the Law. Christ, though born under the Law, was not made a Priest under it, as Aaron was. The change lies in this, that the Levitical priests were made "after the Law of a carnal commandment," but Christ "after the power of an endless life" (lit., an indissoluble life, neither changing not passing away). So there is "a disannulling of the foregoing commandment, and a bringing in thereupon of a better hope, through which we draw nigh to God" (vv. 18, 19). That is to say, the change in both Law and Priesthood is not only constitutional, it is also administrative, not only in character but also in effect. The Law could never make men fit for God, nor bring them nigh to Him. Through Christ both are effected (vv. 11-19).

Fifthly, no oath accompanied the appointment of the Aaronic priesthood. Its transitory character was unsuited to that. Inviolability is an essential feature of Christ's Priesthood. The Divine oath, uttered after the Law (see Psa. 110. 4) "appointeth a Son, perfected for evermore" (vv. 20-28). God's oath confirms the inviolable character of that for which it is given. The Levitical priesthood was purely official, Christ's has a greatness that is Personal. Herein lies its attractiveness.

Sixthly, for this reason Christ has become "the Surety of a better Covenant" (vv 20-22). The measure of the superiority of the New Covenant is the measure of the superiority of the Priesthood of Christ. Human need was not met under the old, it is fully met under the new. God's oath and Christ Himself are the guarantee thereof.

Seventhly, the former priests were many; death prevented their continuance; Christ's Priesthood does not pass from one to another (v. 24). By reason of all this "He is able to save to the uttermost them that draw near to God through Him, seeing He ever liveth to make intercession for them."

Anticipations in the Day of His Flesh.

It may be that in the Gospel narratives intimations are given concerning the Priesthood of our Lord. There is something suggestive in the fact that it was when He was "about thirty years of age" that He was baptized* (Luke 3. 23). This was the age at which the priests, after their consecration, were manifested to the nation (Exod. 29. 35; Lev. 8. 33). While then His baptism was a symbolic anticipation of the

---

*The narrative in verse 23 is to be connected immediately with the account of the baptism rather than with His teaching, as in R.V. The word "to teach" is absent from the original, which reads, "And Jesus Himself was beginning about 30 years," that is, when what has just been narrated took place.

significance of His death and resurrection, and likewise a fulfilment of the Divine obligations under the Law, it was at the same time a ceremonial introduction to His public ministry, which in some respects was anticipative of His present priestly function. The Baptist perhaps gave some intimation of this in saying that, though he knew not Jesus personally, yet he had come baptizing with water in order that He might "be made manifest to Israel" (John 1. 31).

There are other priestly acts of the Lord in the days of His flesh, such as His prayer on the night of the betrayal (John 17). His great act of the offering up of Himself on the Cross was priestly in character. This is made clear in the Epistle to the Hebrews as follows: "Such a High Priest became us...who needeth not daily, like those priests, to offer up sacrifices, first for his own sins, and then for the sins of the people: for this He did once for all, when He offered up Himself."

His Official Glory.

The Lord Jesus entered officially on His High Priesthood when He "sat down on the right hand of God" (Heb. 10. 12). "He glorified not Himself to be made a High Priest." He thrust not Himself into the position. The Father appointed Him (5. 5, 10).

His entire suitability and His efficacy are based on the following facts:

Firstly, on the intrinsic excellence of His Person and His proved sinlessness; He is "holy, guileless and undefiled" (7. 26).

Secondly, upon the fact of His Manhood, "It behoved Him in all things to be made like unto His brethren, that He might be a merciful and faithful High Priest" (2. 17).

Thirdly, upon His sufferings as Man, in the days of His flesh; "having offered up prayers and supplications with strong crying and tears unto Him that was able to save Him out of (see *margin*) death, and having been heard for His godly fear, though He was a Son (literally, and more expressively, "although being Son," as just mentioned in 5. 5), yet learned obedience (*i.e.*, in the experience of doing the Father's will) by the things which He suffered; and having been made perfect (not morally—that He ever was—but officially, by reason of His experiences), He became unto all them that obey Him the Author of eternal Salvation; named of God (*i.e.*, officially appointed) a High Priest after the order of Melchizedek" (5. 7-10). Thus He has knowledge of all human need and trial, of every person and every case.

Fourthly, upon the value of His atoning Sacrifice; "through His own blood He entered in once for all into the holy place" (9. 12). Not that He actually took blood into Heaven; the taking of the blood of animals sacrifices by the Aaronic high priests within the veil on the day of Atonement, symbolized indeed the entire acceptance by God of the perfect sacrifice of Christ, but was not intended to suggest the carrying of literal blood by Christ into Heaven.

Fifthly, upon His Resurrection. He was "separated from sinners, and made higher than the heavens" (7. 26).

Sixthly, upon His relationship with those whom He represents. They are His redeemed, His own possession. They, the sanctified, are one with Him, the Sanctifier; "for which cause He is not ashamed to call them brethren."

Seventhly, His Godhood invests His Priesthood with an incalculable efficacy, for He thus has perfect knowledge of all the claims of Divine righteousness, and maintains them, while at the same time securing the welfare of those on whose behalf He acts.

Eighthly, the character and efficacy of His Priesthood rest upon the validity of the Divine counsels. These are exhibited in the terms of the New Covenant, of which He is the Mediator (9. 15—10. 17). His Priesthood is this shown to be merciful, faithful, sympathetic, authoritative and continuous.

His Intercession.

In all the power and virtue, then, of His own Person and work He ever lives to make intercession* for His people. He enters into all their concerns, their needs, and sorrows, and desires. He offers up their prayers and praises, freed from any imperfections which may characterise them, so that they ascend, like the holy incense in the golden censer, in all the perfume of His own acceptance with the Father. He pleads for their consolation and their welfare. As of old the smoke of the burnt offering mingled with the fragrance of the incense, so His intercession ascends in the savour of His sacrifice on the Cross. Moreover, every request He makes has the force of a claim, it constitutes a veritable petition of right. He, and He alone, in His prayer can say, "Father, I will that..." (John 17. 24). His intercessions never fail in their object. On earth He could say, "Thou hearest Me always" (John 11. 42). What he did for His disciples here below He does still with unwearying constancy. His place has changed, but not His affection.

With such a High Priest acting on our behalf there is no room for unbelief. We are to draw near to the throne of grace "with a true heart in fullness of faith." The apprehension of the

---
*The word *entunkano*, to intercede, primarily signified to fall in with a person; then, to have intimate dealings with him, so as to gain his ear; and hence, to make an entreaty, or interpose on behalf of others.

purpose and value of His ministry will rid us of all self-sufficiency and keep us in self-abasement, and in entire dependence upon His power and mercy. The throne of glory has become a throne of grace. There we "may receive mercy and may find grace." There the believer's cup of comfort is filled to overflowing and the Divine consolations abound in his soul, for the refreshment of his spirit and the renewal of his strength.

CHAPTER XI

The Second Advent.

WHILE the Scriptures set before us the Lord's Return as the hope of believers, it is especially presented as the object of

Christ's Own Expectancy.

The hope is essentially His hope, and we can only rightly experience the power of its anticipation as we so view it. His eager anticipation breathes in His words to the disciples in the upper room: "If I go and prepare a place for you, I come again, and will receive you unto Myself; that where I am ye may be also," and further, in His prayer that follows: "Father I will that they also whom Thou hast given Me be with Me where I am." So again four times in the Book of Revelation His message rings out, "I come quickly," first in the letter addressed to the Church at Philadelphia (chap. 3. 11), and then finally three times at the close of the Book (chap. 22. 7, 12, 20).

His coming to receive the Church to Himself is, however, only the first step in the accomplishment of that for which He waits. For the Rapture of the Church will be but preliminary to a series of events which will culminate in His overthrow of the foes of God, and the setting up of His Kingdom on earth. His expectancy in this respect is frequently brought out in the Gospels, and in the statement in the Epistle to the Hebrews, "He sat down on the right hand of God, from henceforth expecting till His enemies be made the footstool of His feet" (Heb. 10. 13). He cannot be satisfied while the usurper holds sway over the world which He came to redeem. At His Second Advent He will banish this arch-enemy from the scene, take the reins of sovereignty, and, governing the world in righteousness, will at length abolish all rule and all authority and power, and hand over the Kingdom to the Father (1 Cor. 15. 24, 25). In long-suffering patience He waits till the purposes of God for the present age have been accomplished. Probably this was in the Apostle's mind in his desire for the saints in Thessalonica, "The Lord direct your hearts into the love of God and into the patience of Christ" (2 Thess. 3. 5, R.V.), which would thus mean 'the Lord direct your hearts to love as God loves, and to be patient as Christ is patient.'

The Day of Christ.

A clear distinction is made in the Word of God between the circumstances connected with the coming of the Lord to receive the Church to Himself and His coming with the Church and with all His angels, for the execution of Divine retribution upon the foes of God, and for the establishment of His Kingdom in the world. The Resurrection and Rapture of the saints will introduce "the Day of our Lord Jesus Christ" (1 Cor. 1. 8). His coming to the earth in Judgment will introduce "the Day of the Lord" (1 Thess. 5. 2). The former is otherwise called "the Day of Christ" (Phil. 1. 10; 2. 16), "the Day of Jesus Christ" (Phil. 1. 6), "the Day of the Lord Jesus" (1 Cor. 5. 5; 2 Cor. 1. 14). These terms are applied, as the context shows in each case, to the period beginning with the Rapture, when the saints will be with the Lord, and will stand before His Judgment Seat to receive the things done in the body. The Apostle exhorts them, for instance, to be "sincere and void of offence unto the Day of Christ" (Phil. 1. 10). God, who has begun a good work in them, will perform it "unto the Day of Jesus Christ" (chap. 1. 6). He assures the saints at Corinth of the confirming work of God in them, so that they may be "unreproveable in the Day of our Lord Jesus Christ" (1 Cor. 1. 8). Looking forward to the same time he says, "We are your glorying even as ye also are ours in the Day of our Lord Jesus" (2 Cor. 1. 14). Believers are so to live now that they may be "sincere and void of offence unto the Day of Christ" (Phil. 1. 10).

The Second Advent.

The Parousia.

A comparison with similar Scriptures shows that the term "Parousia" is applied to the same scene and circumstances. This term is sometimes rendered "coming," which, however, is not an adequate translation. It signifies literally "a being with," or "presence," and is so rendered, *e.g.*, in Philippians 1. 26; 2. 12. We never read simply of a parousia to persons, but always of a parousia with them. That the Rapture introduces the Parousia of the Lord with His people and that in that period the Judgment Seat of Christ will be set, is clear from what follows. In writing to the Thessalonians Paul uses the term in a way which makes it impossible to view it as applicable merely to the moment of the Lord's descent into the air. He says, "For what is our hope, or joy, or crown of glorying?..Are not even ye, before our Lord Jesus at (or rather "in") His Parousia" (1 Thess. 2. 19). The fruit of the Apostle's service on their behalf will then be seen. Again, he desires that the Lord shall so work in them that they may be "unblameable in holiness, before our Lord and Father, at (lit. "in") the Parousia of our Lord Jesus Christ with all His saints" (chap. 3. 13). Obviously this does not refer to the coming of the Lord in glory with His saints and His holy angels to overthrow His foes, but to the period when the saints will be with Christ after the Rapture. Further, the Apostle desires that God may sanctify them wholly in order that their "whole spirit and soul and body may be preserved entire, without blame, in the Parousia of our Lord Jesus Christ" (chap. 5. 23).

The Apostle John, anticipating the same time, says, "Now my little children, abide in Him; that, if He shall be manifested, we may have boldness, and not be ashamed before Him in His Parousia" (1 John 2. 28). In other words he desires that both he himself, and they who have been the objects of his care, may have boldness and not be ashamed at the Judgment Seat of Christ. Similarly Paul desired that the saints at Philippi should be blameless and harmless, and should shine as lights in the world, that he might have "whereof to glory in the Day of Christ," that he had not run in vain, neither laboured in vain (Phil. 2. 16). For then the work of each shall be made manifest, "for the Day shall declare it," that is, the Day of Christ. That which abides will meet with a reward. "If any man's work shall be burned he shall suffer loss, and he himself shall be saved, yet so as through fire" (1 Cor. 3. 13-15). John desires that his spiritual children shall not lose these things which he had wrought, but that they shall receive a full reward (2 John 8). Then, too, the rewards promised by the Lord Jesus in the second and third chapters of Revelation to those who overcome, will be assigned.

The Day of the Lord.

The phrase "the Day of the Lord" is used in an entirely different connection. It never refers to the events which we have been considering, but relates to the Lord's judgment of the world at His Personal intervention in its affairs, that is to say, to the time when "He shall come in flaming fire, rendering vengeance to them that know not God and to them that obey not the Gospel," and "to be glorified in His saints, and to be marvelled at in all them that believed" (2 Thess. 1. 7-10; cp. Col. 3. 4). The Apostle distinguishes the Day of the Lord from the Parousia, in 2 Thessalonians 2. He writes "touching (or rather, 'in the interests of') the Parousia of our Lord Jesus Christ, and our gathering together unto Him," *i.e.*, at the Rapture. Some confusion had arisen in the minds of the converts between the Parousia and the Day of the Lord since he wrote the first Epistle.* Some were supposing

---

* "That they are distinct periods, the following considerations go to show:
1, "whereas the Day of the Lord is a subject of Old Testament prophecy, the Parousia is not:
2, "the scene of the Day of the Lord is the earth; the scene of the Parousia is the air:
3, "the Day of the Lord, since it is a period of judgment and punishment, is to be anticipated with dread; the Parousia, since it is a period of rest and reward, is to be anticipated with joy:
4, "from the Day of the Lord believers are to be delivered, saved; in the Parousia they are to meet the Lord and be with Him:
5, "angels are prominent in connection with the Day of the Lord; they are not mentioned in connection with the Parousia."
(*Notes on the Epistle to the Thessalonians*, by Hogg and Vine, *p.* 245.)

that the latter period had already begun. He warns them, therefore, not to be deceived into thinking "that the Day of the Lord is now present" (see the R.V., which gives the correct rendering). He had spoken of the Rapture and the Parousia in the First Epistle (chap. 5. 4, *e.g.*), and also of the Day of the Lord. The latter would come "as a thief in the night" and bring "sudden destruction" upon the world (chap. 5. 2, 3). If, then, as they supposed the Day of the Lord had begun, they might well be in perturbation of mind. He now assures them that the Day of the Lord will not take place till two other events have transpired, namely, "the falling away" and the revelation of the Man of Sin. His career of anti-Christian rule will be suddenly terminated by the Lord Jesus Himself, who will slay him "with the breath of His mouth," and bring him to naught "by the manifestation of His coming," literally, "the outshining of His Parousia." That is one and the same event with His revelation from Heaven "with the angels of His power in flaming fire" (chap. 1. 7, 8). The Apostle Paul, to whom especially, it should be remembered, was committed the truth of the Mystery relating to the Rapture (1 Cor. 15. 51), does not teach that certain events must transpire before that takes place.

The Manifestation of the Parousia.

The Epiphany, or shining forth, of the Parousia, which introduces the Day of the Lord, is what Christ spoke of when He said that "as the lightning cometh forth from the east, and is seen even unto the west, so shall be the Coming (or Parousia) of the Son of Man" (Matt. 24. 27). Christ and the saints in resurrection life and glory will then be revealed to the world, which He will come to judge in righteousness. This sudden manifestation of Christ as the Son of Man will terminate the fierce persecution carried on by the Antichrist, a persecution chiefly directed against the Jews. The Lord says that "immediately after the tribulation of those days, the sun shall be darkened, and the moon shall not give her light, and the stars shall fall from Heaven, and the powers of the heavens shall be shaken: and then shall appear the sign of the Son of Man in Heaven; and then shall all the tribes of the earth mourn, and they shall see the Son of Man coming on the clouds of Heaven with power and great glory" (Matt. 24. 29, 30). The phrase "the sign of the Son of Man" is subjective, that is to say, His appearance will be the sign itself.

Luke adds that before this there will be "distress of nations, men fainting for fear and for expectation of the things which are coming on the earth" (Luke 21. 25, 26; compare Acts 2. 20, quoted from Joel 2. 30). These and other passages make clear that the coming of the Son of Man in power and great glory will introduce the Day of the Lord. Perhaps the most vivid description of the details of this intervention are given in Revelation 19. The strife of Armageddon will be hushed to stillness. The Jewish nation will be delivered from its tyrant and his confederates, and from its long period of unbelief. They will look on Him whom they have pierced and mourn and repent. The beast and the false prophet will be cast alive into the Lake of Fire. Satan will be bound for a thousand years and cast into the abyss.

The Marriage and the Marriage Feast.

It would seem that following upon this there will be an earthly celebration of the marriage of the Lamb, which has taken place in Heaven. For before the events just mentioned the announcement is made in Heaven that "the marriage of the Lamb has come,* and His wife has made herself ready. And it was given unto her that she should array herself in fine linen, bright and pure; for the fine linen is the righteous acts of the saints" (chap. 19. 8). For these acts they will have been rewarded. That the celebration of this heavenly union takes place on the earth is indicated in

---

*The tense is the aorist, or past, and signifies that the marriage has taken place.

several places in the Gospels, in each of which the Revised Version rightly gives "the marriage feast" instead of "the marriage" or "wedding." See the Revised Version of Matthew 22. 2, 3, 4, 9. Thus it is from an earthly scene that the man without the wedding garment is cast into the outer darkness. See also Matthew 25. 10 and Luke 12. 36.

The Judgment of the Nations.

Again, it is when the Son of Man comes in His glory and all the holy angels with Him, that He will sit on the Throne of His glory, and the nations of the world will be gathered together to be judged before Him (Matt. 25. 32-46). The kingdom of the world will have become "the Kingdom of our Lord and Saviour Jesus Christ, and He shall reign for ever and ever" (Rev. 11. 15). Sin, however, will not be eradicated from the earth during the Millennial period. Even the personal presence of Christ, and the establishment of His Kingdom will not accomplish the regeneration of the human heart. That alone can be effected on the ground of His Death.

The Millennium.

At the end of the first century of the Millennium a generation will have arisen which will know only Millennial experience, and will therefore be familiar only with the circumstances of the world's peace, and of the absolutely righteous and firm government of the King of kings. At the close of this period, therefore, there will be a large number who will yield ready allegiance to the Evil One, when he is permitted to make his final attempt against God. Then, and not till then, will every enemy be subdued. Christ must reign "till He has put all His enemies under His feet." Then He will deliver up the Kingdom of God, even the Father; when He shall have abolished all rule and all authority and all power." "And when all things have been subjected unto Him, then shall the Son also Himself be subjected to Him that did subject all things unto Him, that God may be all and in all" (1 Cor. 15. 24-28).

www.ingramcontent.com/pod-product-compliance
Lightning Source LLC
Chambersburg PA
CBHW060405090426
42734CB00011B/2267